HUME'S INTENTIONS

HUME'S INTENTIONS

JOHN PASSMORE

*Professor of Philosophy in the
Australian National University*

THIRD EDITION

DUCKWORTH

Third edition (with appendix) 1980
First published (by Cambridge University Press) 1952
Second Edition (Duckworth) 1968

Gerald Duckworth & Co. Ltd
The Old Piano Factory
43 Gloucester Crescent
London NW1

© 1968, 1980 *by* JOHN PASSMORE

ISBN 0 7156 0918 1 (cased)

British Library Cataloguing in Publication Data

Passmore, John
  Hume's Intentions. — 3rd ed.
  1. Hume, David
  I. Title
  192   B1498

  ISBN 0-7156-0918-1

PRINTED IN GREAT BRITAIN
BY UNWIN BROTHERS LIMITED
THE GRESHAM PRESS, OLD WOKING, SURREY

CONTENTS

v

PREFACE TO THE THIRD EDITION

WHEN I wrote the first edition of this book my eye, as was the custom of the time, was on the thrust of the argument rather than on scholarly niceties. Mr E. J. Khamara, of Monash University, was good enough to draw attention to a number of points at which citations had gone awry; my wife, scrutinising the text, found several more. These I have corrected where they could possibly have been a source of error or confusion. It is still true that I have modernised quotations more than I should now permit myself to do and have not always sufficiently indicated minor lacunae in quotations. But the cost of alterations being what it is I have for the most part had to allow such lapses to remain untouched, except where they were likely to be misleading.

Fully to have taken into account the recent literature on Hume would have been to write a new book, which would not then have been the work to which so many later commentators have generously alluded. But I have added an appendix on 'Hume and the Ethics of Belief', a substantially revised version of an essay first published in G. P. Morice (ed.): *David Hume: Bicentenary Papers*. My thanks are due, for permission to do so, to the Edinburgh University Press and the Texas University Press.

Canberra, 1979. J. P.

PREFACE TO THE FIRST EDITION

BOOKS ought not to be multiplied except of necessity; commentaries on Hume have flourished so exceedingly, and even excessively, that the present work might seem to flout that admirable general principle. In extenuation, I should explain that this is not a commentary, that it in no way supersedes Laird's *Hume's Philosophy of Human Nature* or Kemp Smith's *Philosophy of David Hume* but seeks rather to complement them. I have not tried to write a page-by-page account of Hume's philosophy; my object has been to disentangle certain main themes in that philosophy and to show how they are related to Hume's main philosophic purpose, in the expectation that an account of the way in which he develops these themes will be philosophically as well as historically enlightening. Criticism and scholarship are intermingled, out of a conviction that criticism without scholarship is cavilling, and scholarship without criticism is pedantry. The book has, I hope, a unity. At the same time, since some readers will no doubt be interested in one of these themes rather than another, I have tried to make each chapter a relatively independent discussion, even at the cost of occasional repetition.

My interest in Hume was first aroused by the lectures of Professor John Anderson, Professor of Philosophy in the University of Sydney, and his pupils will recognize that I am much indebted to him, especially perhaps in the second chapter but in one way and another throughout the whole book. But my method of interpretation is not his; it was first suggested to me by Professor N. Kemp Smith's articles on 'The Naturalism of Hume' (*Mind*, Nos. 54-5); for some time my work ran parallel with his, as I discovered from his *Philosophy of David Hume*; I owe a great deal to that book, to his edition of Hume's *Dialogues on Natural Religion*, and to his personal encouragement. Of my other predecessors, John Laird and T. H. Green are the ones to whom I feel myself most indebted, but I have borrowed copiously from innumerable sources. A number of friends, colleagues and students have been good enough to read one or other of the earlier versions of this book; if I single out two, Professor Gilbert Ryle and Mr Denis Grey, it is because they proved my most troublesome and therefore most rewarding critics. Mr R. Durrant freed the text of a great many blemishes by his careful scrutiny of the proofs; my wife added to her other trials by helping with the index and proof correction. If errors remain, it is only because no one can fully protect me against the consequences of my own carelessness.

For the rest, I should like to express my gratitude to the

library staff of the University of Otago for its patience when confronted by my constant demands upon its time, and to the Research Committee of the University of New Zealand and the Arts Research Committee of the University of Sydney for their financial assistance, which so greatly facilitated the writing of this book. Finally, but not least, I should like to thank my wife, my family, and my colleagues for not only submitting for so long a time to my preoccupation with Hume but even encouraging it, by relieving me of tasks which would otherwise have fallen to my lot.

J. P.

University of Otago,
November 1951

PREFACE TO THE SECOND EDITION

FOR reasons of economy, I have not been able to make any considerable alterations to the text of this new edition. But I have corrected the text at points where correction was obviously called for, in the light of subsequent scholarship, and have added an additional note to the second chapter. Were I now to rewrite the book afresh, I should particularly concentrate my attention on that chapter, and the reader should, I now think, read it last rather than second. But I still believe that the views it contains deserve consideration, although they are too lightly sketched to be immediately convincing. I hope eventually to expand them in a different, and more suitable, context.

Canberra, 1968   J. P.

ABBREVIATIONS

THE following abbreviations and short titles are used:

T, 1: Hume's *Treatise of Human Nature*, ed. L. A. Selby-Bigge (Oxford, 1896), page 1.

E, 1: Hume's *Enquiries concerning the Human Understanding and Concerning the Principles of Morals*, ed. L. A. Selby-Bigge (Oxford, 2nd ed., 1902), page 1.

G.G., 1, 1: *The Philosophical Works of David Hume*, ed. T. H. Green and T. H. Grose (London, 1874), vol. 1, page 1.

A, 1: Hume's *An Abstract of a Treatise on Human Nature*, ed. J. M. Keynes and P. Sraffa (Cambridge, 1938), page 1.

D, 1: Hume's *Dialogues Concerning Natural Religion*, ed. N. Kemp Smith (London, 2nd ed., 1947), page 1.

Letters, 1, 1: *The Letters of David Hume*, ed. J. Y. T. Greig (Oxford, 1932), vol. 1, page 1.

Recherche, 1, 1: Malebranche's *Recherche de la Vérité*, éd. Flammarion (Paris, n.d.), vol. 1, page 1.

References to the works of Descartes are to the translation by E. S. Haldane and G. R. T. Ross, second edition, Cambridge, 1931, in two volumes.

References to Newton's *Principia Mathematica* are to the edition translated by Andrew Motte and edited by W. Davis, in three volumes (London, 1803) ; references to his *Opticks* are to the fourth edition, London, 1730, reprinted by George Bell and Sons, London, 1931.

CHAPTER I

IN DEFENCE OF THE MORAL SCIENCES

HUME is one of the most exasperating of philosophers. Each separate sentence in his writings—with very few exceptions—is admirable in its lucidity: the tangled syntax and barbarous locutions which bedevil the reader of Kant and Hegel are completely absent. And yet, although in a different way, Hume is at least as difficult as Hegel. In his editorial introduction to the *Enquiries*, Selby-Bigge summed up the Hume problem thus: 'He says so many different things in so many different ways and different connexions, and with so much indifference to what he has said before, that it is very hard to say positively that he taught or did not teach this or that particular doctrine. . . . This makes it easy to find all philosophies in Hume or, by setting up one statement against another, none at all.'

Faced with inconsistencies on this scale, the interpreter may proceed in one of a number of ways. Most boldly, he may denounce Hume's philosophy as a mere hotch-potch which has achieved its present reputation only because muddle and confusion have a fatal fascination—a conclusion which few have adopted but by which many more must have been tempted. Or, at the opposite extreme, he may argue that Hume's inconsistencies are but peccadillos, deriving in part from the tendency of innovators to fall back, in careless moments, upon the doctrines they have elsewhere demolished, in part from Hume's youthfulness; he had not acquired that mature cunning which teaches men to conceal their hesitations and to gloss over inconvenient facts. Neither of these methods of interpretation ought to be dismissed as merely absurd: the first reminds us that Hume was sometimes a very bad philosopher, whom no amount of piety can extenuate; the second, that in the writings of a youthful innovator accidental inconsistencies will be unusually frequent and blatant.

Yet neither interpretation is finally satisfactory. Hume's influence on the history of philosophy has not been entirely calamitous; if he is sometimes a bad philosopher, on other occasions he is a remarkably good one. And, on the other side, the inconsistencies in his philosophy cut too deep to be dismissed as unimportant. If we try to show that Hume is really a phenomenalist, or a sceptic, or a naturalist, and that those sections of his work which will not fit into such a single philosophical system are no more than slips of the pen, we shall have to admit that his 'slips' are of gigantic proportions; and we shall be quite baffled by the way in which he not merely falls into, but goes out of his way to develop and extol, views which are quite incompatible with whatever systematic doctrine we care to ascribe to him.

To avoid such general problems of interpretation, we might prefer to select from Hume's work whatever we choose to regard as philosophically important, perhaps his theory of causality or his theory of the external world, leaving aside as of merely historical interest the question what, in general, Hume was trying to do. On the face of it, this is a reasonable enough procedure; but whenever it has been attempted it has given rise to 'replies to Hume' which quite miss the force of his argument, or to 'developments of his view' along precisely those lines which Hume has shown to be impossible. There are organic connexions which we sever at the cost of misunderstanding between the different segments of Hume's theory.

The interpretation now to be embarked upon tries to bring out the nature of these connexions, while at the same time not attempting to describe Hume' work by any single philosophical epithet. To call him a naturalist, a phenomenalist or a sceptic would be seriously misleading; we should add that he is an anti-naturalist, an anti-phenomenalist and an anti-sceptic. Yet for all that, there is a unity in his work; it is dominated by a single over-riding intention.

Hume's intentions, according to a familiar legend, were of a distinctly dishonourable kind. He tells us himself that his ruling passion was a 'love of literary fame'[1]; but that, according

[1] *My Own Life* (reprinted in *Letters*, Vol. I).

to his detractors, is too favourable a description of his motives. 'Hume exhibits no small share of the craving after mere notoriety and vulgar success as distinct from the pardonable, if not honourable, ambition for solid and enduring fame, which would have harmonized better with his philosophy.' These are the magisterial words of T. H. Huxley, but this same interpretation of Hume's intentions was the delight of his more bigoted contemporaries and still persists in our own time.[1]

It is particularly invoked to explain why, as the charge is commonly formulated, Hume 'abandoned philosophy' after the *Treatise*, 'turning to those political and historical topics which were likely to yield, and did in fact yield a much better return of that sort of success which his soul loved'.[2] The *Treatise* had not the stuff of notoriety in it, and so he turned his attention away from philosophy to theology and moral science. 'Since he couldn't shock men by a new theory of science, he would try politics and religion.'[3]

We are not now concerned to defend Hume's personal character; the importance of the legend, to us, is that it rests upon a misapprehension of Hume's intentions in the *Treatise*, a misapprehension which extends beyond the ranks of his denigrators. Hume, it is supposed, set out to write a 'critical philosophy'; his intention, if we may so express the matter, was to be a precursor to Kant. He came to recognize that his philosophy was in certain respects defective; as a good philosopher, he should have busied himself with the removal of these defects. Instead, in the *Enquiries* he is content to leave out what he should be reconsidering; and in the rest of his writings he abandons even this mitigated and vulgarized philosophy for history, politics and economics. No one concerned for the truth, the presumption is, could so lightly abandon philosophy for the frivolities of the social sciences.

Now, even the sub-title of the *Treatise* is enough to rule out

[1] The Huxley quotation is from his *Hume*, p. 11. For a thorough and decisive criticism of the Hume legend, see E. C. Mossner, 'Philosophy and Biography: The Case of David Hume' (*Philosophical Review*, April 1950). [2] Huxley, *loc. cit.*

[3] J. H. Randall Jnr. on 'David Hume: Radical Empiricist and Pragmatist' in *Freedom and Experience* (ed. S. Hook and M. R. Konvitz), p. 294.

this misinterpretation; the *Treatise* is there described as 'an attempt to introduce the experimental method of reasoning into moral subjects'. This is a clear indication that Hume's major interest, from the very beginning, was in 'moral subjects'. ('The moral subjects'—in contrast with *physical* subjects—are those which together make up what Hume calls 'the science of man', i.e. the science which concerns itself with the human mind and with human relationships in society. The subjects Hume used as defining examples are ethics, politics, criticism and logic—the latter conceived as the 'art of reasoning'. He does not use the word 'psychology', which was introduced into English by Hartley.) Hume's choice of examples is equally significant. In Book I of the *Treatise*, he exemplifies a causal chain thus: 'cousins in the fourth degree are connected by causation . . . but not so closely as brothers, much less as child and parent' (T, 11). And he goes on to illustrate the metaphysical distinction between power and its exercise by referring to the relationship between a political authority and its subjects. A passage in the *Dissertation* is even more revealing. 'Property', he there writes, 'is a species of causation. . . . It is indeed the relation the most interesting of any, and occurs the most frequently to the mind'.[1] Almost certainly, this is not an example which would naturally be employed by the ordinary philosopher; if examples of this sort are 'the most interesting', this is only because Hume himself was most interested in them.

But we need not have recourse to psychological analysis; he tells us himself, plainly enough, that the moral sciences are the only ones worth studying. 'In these four sciences of Logic, Morals, Criticism and Politics', he writes in the Preface of the *Treatise*, 'is comprehended almost every thing, which it can any way import us to be acquainted with' (T, xix). At the very end of Book I, after all his philosophical vicissitudes, he insists on the same point. His intention, as he there expresses it, is to give 'in some particulars a different turn to the speculations of philosophers' by 'pointing out to them more distinctly those

[1] G.G., IV, 151n. This note was not added until the 1760 edition, but the doctrine that property is a species of causation was already taught in the *Treatise* (T, 310).

subjects, where alone they can expect assurance and conviction'
(T, 273), those subjects, namely, which are incorporated in 'the
science of man'. He mentions his predecessors—'Mr. Locke,
my Lord Shaftesbury, Dr. Mandeville, Mr. Hutchinson (*sic*),
Dr. Butler etc.' (T, xxi)—not, be it observed, Bishop Berkeley.
There can be no doubt that (like many another philosopher)
Hume came to be more interested in politics and less in
philosophy, in the modern sense of that word, as he grew older.
But the moral sciences had been his principal concern even
when he was writing Book I of the *Treatise*.

In this respect, Hume was a child of his age. We now think
of the late seventeenth and early eighteenth centuries as a period
peculiarly rich in physicists and philosophers. But it must not
be forgotten that Wollaston was read, when Berkeley and Hume
were spurned as 'eccentrics', and that Locke's reputation
depended on his psychology rather than on his logic (as we can
see clearly enough in *Tristram Shandy*). Even those who most
admired the genius of Newton still deprecated any emphasis
on physical science. Pope's attitude is typical. In his *Epitaph
on Sir Isaac Newton* he could write:

> Nature and Nature's Laws lay hid in night;
> God said, Let Newton be! and all was light

but the lesson of the *Essay on Man* is that

> . . . all our knowledge is, Ourselves to know

and Newton is put in his place:

> Could he, whose rules the rapid comet bind,
> Describe or fix one movement of his mind?[1]

The same lesson was taught by Malebranche, so often Hume's
teacher. 'La plus belle, la plus agréable et la plus nécessaire
de toutes nos connaissances est sans doute la connaissance de
nous-mêmes. De toutes les sciences humaines, la science de
l'homme est la plus digne de l'homme. Cependant, cette
science n'est pas la plus cultivée ni la plus achevée que nous
ayons; le commun des hommes la neglige entièrement.'[2]

[1] The first quotation from the *Essay on Man* is Epistle IV, line 398, the
second is Epistle I, lines 35-6.　　　[2] *Recherche*, Vol. I, p. xiii.

Why, then, did Hume write Book I of the *Treatise*? Why did he not embark immediately on 'the moral subjects'? Even if, as he says, he 'cannot forbear having a curiosity to be acquainted with the principles of moral good and evil, the nature and foundation of government, and the cause of those several passions and inclinations, which actuate and govern me' (T, 271), it is not immediately clear how this curiosity can be, as he says it is, 'the origin of (his) philosophy', a philosophy so much concerned with topics of a purely logical kind.

The moral sciences, Hume thought, stood in need of a new logic : to supply that logic is the main intention behind Book I of the *Treatise*. Without anachronism, we can think of it as Hume's methodology of the social sciences. Hume shared the Cartesian attitude to syllogism; the old logic would not do. He fully sympathized with Descartes' attempt to state a few simple rules of method, which would 'comprise the advantages' of the traditional logic, while being 'exempt from its faults'.[1] However, the Cartesian logic would not do either; understood 'in a reasonable sense', it could be a distinct aid to enquiry, but it relied upon self-evident premises, which are entirely lacking, Hume argues, in any empirical science (E, 150). On this point, Hartley was the Cartesian; he looked forward to a day when 'future generations shall put all kinds of evidence and enquiries into mathematical forms . . . so as to make mathematics and logic, natural history and civil history, natural philosophy and philosophy of all other kinds, coincide *omni ex parte*'.[2] Much impressed by de Moivre's theory of chances, Hartley concluded that all reasoning could be mathematized by the use of the logic of chances. This is precisely what Hume took to be impossible.

Hume thought he could show that the certainty attaching to mathematics (concerned as it was with 'relations of ideas') could never be extended to the 'matters of fact' of the social and physical sciences. It is true that in one essay, *That Politics May be Reduced to a Science*, he suggested that 'so great is the force of laws and of particular forms of government . . . that

[1] *Discourse on Method* (Vol. 1, p. 92).
[2] *Observations on Man*, Proposition LXXXVII.

consequences almost as certain and general may sometimes be deduced from them, as any which the mathematical sciences afford us.'[1] But this must be a rhetorical gesture: and even in the full flow of his rhetoric Hume could not bring himself to omit the restrictive 'almost'. Supposing now that the moral sciences do not possess the certainty of mathematics, the question is how they can have any 'foundations' whatsoever. Descartes had argued that there was no third way between recognizing the 'certainty' of science and falling into absolute scepticism. Locke, however, had already embarked, somewhat unsteadily, on a theory of 'judgment', defined as a 'twilight state' between ignorance and 'clear and certain knowledge';[2] and Butler (whose opinion of the *Treatise* Hume so anxiously sought) had drawn attention to the need for a logic of analogy.[3] But Hume refers us specifically to Leibniz, who, he says, 'has observed it to be a common defect in the common systems of logic that they are very copious when they explain the operations of the understanding in the forming of demonstrations, but are too concise when they treat of probabilities, and those other measures of evidence on which life and action entirely depend, and which are our guides even in most of our philosophical speculations' (A, 7). Hume makes it perfectly clear in the *Abstract* that he thought he had remedied this defect in traditional logic. In his methodological moods, then, he thinks of himself as establishing the possibility of a *via media* between Cartesianism and scepticism by laying down rules for deciding what is probable; these rules are needed, because the social sciences cannot hope to achieve absolute certainty, and must work, therefore, with a logic of probability.

The moral sciences were defective, then, because they lacked a satisfactory 'art of reasoning'; this defect they shared with every empirical science. In certain other respects, they lagged behind physics. Hobbes had already complained that men wrote about ethics as rhetoricians rather than as scientists.[4] When he was a young man of twenty-three, Hume wrote to his

[1] G.G., III, 99.   [2] *Essay*, Bk. IV, Ch. xiv.
[3] *Analogy of Religion*, Introduction.   For Hume's anxiety, see *Letters*, Vol. I, p. 27.   [4] *De Corpore*, Book I, Ch. i, 7.

physician, in an equally critical spirit, that 'the moral philosophy transmitted to us by antiquity laboured under the same
inconvenience that has been found in their natural philosophy,
of being entirely hypothetical, and depending more upon
invention than experience' (L, 1, 16). In short, moral science
had yet to experience its Newtonian revolution.

Thus Hume's second task as a methodologist was to show that
the Newtonian 'methods of philosophizing' are as applicable in
the moral as they are in the physical sciences. Hypotheses
could be dispensed with, in so far, at least, as hypotheses are
occult qualities; experience must be the arbiter. Let us ask,
always, whether an expression refers to an idea or an impression;
if the answer is 'an idea', we must seek the impression from
which it is derived. 'This', he says, 'will immediately cut off all
loose discourses and declamations, and reduce us to something precise and exact on the present subject' (T, 456).
General laws must be propounded, on the model of the
Newtonian laws of gravitation; Hume thought he could point
to such laws in the form of associative principles, which 'are
really to *us* the cement of the universe' (A, 32). In the end,
perhaps, his enthusiasm for the Newtonian method somewhat
diminished,[1] but it is a most important thread in the *Treatise*.

It was, of course, a serious question whether the methods
of science could properly be applied to moral subjects. Beattie
was to argue, in a manner still familiar, that if we seek a
'moral writer of true genius' we should look amongst the poets
rather than amongst the philosophers, that 'a metaphysician,
exploring the recesses of the human heart, has just such a chance
for finding the truth, as a man with microscopic eyes would have
for finding the road'.[2] And Beattie can be relied upon to
express the commonplace view. Thus Hume had to show not
only how the moral sciences should be conducted, but even
that they could be conducted at all.

[1] cf. N.Kemp Smith, *The Philosophy of David Hume, passim*; although I shall
be suggesting that Kemp Smith somewhat underrates the vitality, in Hume's
thinking, of the Newtonian approach. He met with Newton's ideas when he
was a very young man at Edinburgh University (cf. Mossner's *Life*) from his
teachers there.
[2] *Essay on Truth*, p. 401 (Seventh Edition).

Paradoxically, it is his defence of the moral sciences which leads Hume most deeply into scepticism. He begins from the common objection to the moral sciences that, to use modern language, they 'involve judgments of value', and hence that we cannot expect, within them, the objectivity which we rightly demand of physical science. Hutcheson had particularly insisted that moral and aesthetic judgments rest on 'feeling' rather than on pure observation or rational deduction; Hume, as Kemp Smith has pointed out,[1] tries to show that Hutcheson's analysis can be applied to every judgment, to natural philosophy no less than to ethics and aesthetics. Thus the supposed superior objectivity of the physical sciences completely vanishes; every judgment is equally 'subjective', every belief rests on taste and sentiment. ''Tis not solely in poetry and music, we must follow our taste and sentiment, but likewise in philosophy' (T, 103).[2] When this intention is dominant, Hume's philosophy drops to its most sceptical level: 'after the most accurate and exact of my reasonings, I can give no reason

---

[1] *Philosophy of David Hume*, p. 43.

[2] The word 'philosophy' is used by seventeenth and eighteenth century writers in three different although closely connected ways (cf. E. Gilson's edition of Descartes' *Discours de la Méthode*, p. 275). First, as meaning enquiry in general, what Descartes calls 'l'étude de la Sagesse' and Berkeley, 'the study of wisdom and truth' (*Principles*, Introduction § 1). This is a translation of Cicero's 'studium sapientiae' (*De Officiis*, II, ii, 5). Cicero's definition, according to the O.E.D., 'was considered authoritative'. Secondly, as meaning the theory which concerns itself with first principles (the scholastic *philosophia prima*). Thirdly, as meaning any one of what we now call the sciences, sometimes with a prefix ('natural philosophy', 'moral philosophy'), sometimes with no such prefix. Hume calls Locke and Malebranche 'philosophers' (E, 7), but equally it is a 'philosopher' (without the appendage of 'natural') who 'determined the laws and forces, by which the revolutions of the planets are governed and directed' (E, 14). As early as 1661, Joseph Glanvill in *The Vanity of Dogmatising* (p. 236) had suggested the word 'science' as a name for 'that part of philosophy which concerns itself with Nature', but the distinction between science and philosophy had no point until the doctrine had gained ground that science gave a complete account of phenomena but left ultimates, or reasons why, or Reality, to philosophy. In the present instance, Hume seems to be using 'philosophy' to mean 'enquiry into matters of fact', including therefore the physical sciences, but also the moral sciences and therefore those parts of metaphysics which are not totally void of content. And this is his ordinary use of the word. We must never read 'philosophy', in the contemporary manner, as 'non-scientific'. Malebranche and Cudworth, Newton and Harvey, in so far as they are not talking nonsense or mathematics, are 'philosophers'.

why I should assent to it; and feel nothing but a *strong* propensity to consider objects *strongly* in that view, under which they appear to me' (T, 265).

Yet to this conclusion he never for long adheres. There is something about *his* propensities which lifts them far above the propensities, however strong, of the metaphysicians and the religious enthusiast. Physics is only a matter of 'sentiment', when it is necessary to deflate the superiority of physicists; the fact remains that it is thoroughly rational, when we contrast it with the vagaries of superstition. The tension generated by these conflicting purposes is most clearly apparent in Hume's embarrassment about his theory of belief, a theory to which he several times returns in the Appendix to the *Treatise*. There is, he says, one observation which he cannot 'forbear': that the difference between 'a poetical enthusiasm' and 'a serious conviction' arises from 'reflexion and *general rules*' (T, 631). 'General rules'—Hume's positive, Newtonian methodology— are to protect us against falling into Protagorean relativism, even though the belief in them, too, is only 'a species of sensation'. The problem is to formulate a logic which will leave room for taste and sentiment without giving any encouragement to the visionary, to develop a scepticism deep enough to dispel the presumption that a developed science will be purely 'rational', but sufficiently 'mitigated' to allow of the supremacy of science over superstition. Hume's inconsistencies arise, in large part, out of his attempt to formulate such a logic and to defend such a scepticism; they are philosophically interesting inconsistencies just because they bear witness to the existence of a genuine problem, and one that still concerns us—how to describe the reasonableness of science without falling into either scepticism or rationalism.

The direction of Hume's thought becomes clear at the end of the first *Enquiry*. There we find him saying of morals and criticism that they 'are not so properly objects of the understanding as of taste and sentiment', and must therefore be contrasted with 'politics, natural philosophy, physics, chemistry etc.' which employ 'moral [i.e. probable] reasoning' *as distinct from* 'taste and sentiment' (E, 165). His development of Hutcheson, according to which moral reasoning itself rests on taste and sentiment, does not really suit Hume's book. In the end, he is prepared to abandon ethics and aesthetics to the realm of taste, if only he can preserve the status of politics, as a science at least as securely founded as physics. But that division between morals and politics formed no part of his original intention: at first, he thought of all the moral sciences as being equally vulnerable, and it is a principal aim of his general logical theory to protect all of them against the criticisms of the rationalist.

There is another aspect, apart from their supposed 'subjectivity', in which the moral might be adjudged inferior to the physical sciences: the physical sciences, it might be argued, penetrate to the real nature of physical objects, whereas the moral sciences have a subject-matter whose real nature we are incapable of discerning. To this criticism, Hume has two lines of reply. The first, the more moderate one, he derives from Locke. The real essences of bodies are quite as unknown to us as the real essences of minds. 'If this impossibility of explaining ultimate principles should be esteemed a defect in the science of man, I will venture to affirm, that it is a defect common to it with all the sciences and all the arts' (T, xxii). It is true that there are certain special difficulties in the social sciences, difficulties in experimenting (in the modern sense of that word), but if we rely upon 'a cautious observation of human life', we shall be able 'to establish a science, which will not be inferior in certainty, and will be much superior in utility to any other of human comprehension'. In passage after passage of the *Treatise* and the *Enquiry* Hume speaks the language of Locke, contrasting the 'real essences' which we do not know with the 'appearances' which we do know, in order to insist that our ignorance of 'true causes' should not be particularly alleged as a defect in the moral sciences.

The second line of defence passes to the attack. Not only need the moral sciences fear no comparison with the physical sciences, but, in fact, the science of man stands pre-eminent, as the foundation upon which all science rests, the true *scientia scientiarum*. 'There is no question of importance, whose decision is not compriz'd in the science of man; and there is none, which can be decided with any certainty, before we become acquainted with that science' (T, xx). To establish this pre-eminence is one of the most important of Hume's intentions, affecting the structure of his argument at point after point.

Mediaeval philosophers had been much concerned to show that the various branches of philosophy fall naturally into a certain order; gradually that view of the matter came to be traditional which is summarized by Descartes in his introduction to *The Principles of Philosophy*. 'Philosophy', wrote Descartes, 'is like a tree whose roots are metaphysics, whose trunk is physics, and whose branches, which arise from this trunk, are all the other sciences.' Hume sets out to show that the theory of human nature, not metaphysics, is the roots and that the moral sciences, not physics, are the trunk. This is the principal intent of his positivism. Metaphysics, he argues, is in part nonsense, in part psychology in disguise—it is nonsense when it talks about essences, occult qualities and the like; it is psychology when it concerns itself with causality, substance, identity. Thus, for example, the metaphysician professes to describe the nature of necessary connexion and to demonstrate that every event has a cause. But on Hume's view this task, as the metaphysician conceives it, is an impossible one; all he can hope to do is to describe the way in which we come to believe that one thing is necessarily connected with another—which is just descriptive psychology. Hume's analysis of causality is a paradigm of philosophy as he would like it to be; *true* metaphysics—the science of human nature, the genuinely fundamental science—replaces false, or visionary, metaphysics. But he is driven into desperate straits when he tries to apply the same kind of analysis to identity, substance and continuity. The inconsistencies which now abound arise directly out of the deficiencies of a psychologistic metaphysics, deficiencies to which Hume himself, in candid moods, draws our attention.

The moral sciences, Hume always presumes, obviously rest upon the science of human nature; and logic, as we have already seen, is included as a species of moral science. Thus he is bound to argue that logical relationships are reducible to psychological connexions; like metaphysical categories, logical constants are associative links, or combinations of such links. Indeed, metaphysics and logic come together, inasmuch as causal connexion, to Hume, is not a physical link but the most important method of inference. *Formal* logic must therefore be discarded—a project which leads to difficulties of overwhelming proportions, but which, once more, sharpens the issues, in this case by helping us to see just how impossible it is to define logic as 'the art of reasoning'.

Since the moral sciences are fundamental, they should clearly be tackled first; afterwards we may 'proceed at leisure to discover more fully those, which are the objects of pure curiosity' (T, xx). But we shall still have need of the science of man: 'even mathematics, natural philosophy, and natural religion, are in some measure dependent on the science of man; since they lie under the cognizance of men, and are judged of, by their powers and faculties.'

On the face of it, this conclusion does not follow; from the fact that all physicists are human beings, it cannot be immediately deduced that an improved knowledge of human beings would be to the advantage of our physics. Hume is relying on an ancillary doctrine, Cartesian in inspiration, viz. that all we are directly acquainted with are 'perceptions of the human mind'. 'Natural Philosophy' must therefore be either a construction out of, or a conjecture from (Hume prefers the latter, Lockian, view to the first, the Berkeleian one), certain of the events which occur in our own minds. If this is true, the more we know about these events the better; that it is true Hume scarcely bothers to affirm, for that was one point on which philosophers agreed. Descartes had maintained that 'the human mind is more easily known than the body'. 'Even bodies', he argues, 'are not properly speaking known by the senses . . . but by the understanding only, and since they are not known from the fact that they are seen or touched, but only because they are understood, I see clearly that there is nothing which is easier for me to know than my own mind.'[1] Hume would not approve of this language, but his line of reasoning is essentially the same. We know directly nothing

[1] *Second Meditation* (Vol. 1, p. 157).

but our perceptions, these perceptions together constitute the human mind, therefore mind alone can be directly experienced.

When Hume emphasizes that natural philosophy employs 'the powers or faculties' of man, this is reminiscent of Locke's starting-point: unless we are first assured of the reliability of our faculties, we can know nothing else, and only an investigation of the understanding can give us that assurance. In the *Enquiry*, Hume rejects such 'antecedent scepticism', on the ground that it involves an infinite regress, since any such inquiry must make use of those very faculties which are supposed to lie under suspicion (E, 150). But this kind of scepticism plays a significant part in establishing the priority of the science of man; if Hume comes to dislike it, this is because it threatens the science of man quite as much as any other science.

For Hume is anxious to maintain that we have no reason to be sceptical, providing we restrict ourselves to the study of man. Then, and only then, can we really know what we are doing. 'So long as we confine our speculations to trade, or morals, or politics, or criticism, we make appeals, every moment, to common sense and experience' (D, 135). He feels obliged to admit, discussing political science, that 'irregular and extraordinary appearances are frequently discovered in the moral, as well as in the physical world',[1] so that, for all the near-mathematical certainty of politics, we must watch our step in formulating general maxims. Still, although we cannot always predict them, we can at least account for such appearances *after* they happen 'from springs and principles, of which everyone has, within himself, or from [obvious] observation, the strongest assurance and conviction'. And when we concern ourselves with the analysis of the human mind itself, as distinct from its activities in trade and politics, we can feel even more confident. This is a point on which Hume regularly insists. 'The intellectual world, tho' involved in infinite obscurities is not perplex'd with any such contradictions, as those we have discover'd in the natural' (T, 232). The reasonings, 'or rather

[1] *Of Some Remarkable Customs*, G.G., III, 374.

conjectures', of physics lead us into 'contradictions and absurdities' whereas 'the perceptions of the mind are perfectly known' (T, 366). Here scepticism must call a halt: 'Nor can there remain any suspicion, that this science is uncertain and chimerical; unless we should entertain such a scepticism as is entirely subversive of all speculation, and even action' (E, 13). That is why Hume is so particularly perturbed by his difficulty in giving an account of personal identity. Principles which cannot be reconciled are grist to his mill when they arise within physics—the light of the moral sciences shines the brighter by contrast. But antinomies in the science of man itself are another, and a really serious, matter. Hume can only hope that 'others, perhaps, or myself upon more mature reflexions, may discover some hypothesis, that will reconcile those contradictions'. Such a reconciliation he would by no means welcome, when the contradictions lie elsewhere.

Hume's main object, then, in Book I of the *Treatise* is to show that the moral sciences can be established on a secure footing. This involves the formulation of a general theory of probable inference, which must leave room for the employment of taste and sentiment, while at the same time excluding, as unscientific, the arguments of the metaphysician and the fancies of the enthusiast. Hume's positivism arises out of his attempt to develop a non-metaphysical, non-declamatory moral science; his phenomenalism serves to buttress the doctrine that the science of man is primarily and pre-eminently secure; his scepticism is intended as a rebuke to physicists and metaphysicians. But he argues beyond his brief; his achievements and his intentions do not wholly coincide.

In the light of this interpretation, let us re-examine the Hume legend. In the *Treatise* he had completed, so he tells us, 'what regards logic' (A, 7); this part of his ambitious schemes for a science of man had been brought to a successful conclusion. If the world paid no attention to his achievement, this could only be because his literary skill was defective. In this critical judgment on the *Treatise*, Hume did not stand alone. 'The style of *The Treatise of Human Nature*', wrote Beattie, 'is so obscure and uninteresting, that if the author had not in his *Essays* republished the capital doctrines of that work, in a more elegant and sprightly manner, a confutation of them would have been altogether unnecessary: their uncouth and gloomy aspect would have deterred most people from courting their acquaintance.'¹ 'An elegant and sprightly manner'—that style Hume employed in the *Enquiries*, not because he was corrupted by his notorious 'love of literary fame', but simply in an effort to make his doctrines intelligible to an audience dominated by the ideal of 'elegance'. When he wrote the first two books of the *Treatise*, Hume, from his French retreat, thought of England as a country 'where all the abstruser sciences are study'd with a peculiar ardour and application' (T, 259); by the time he came to write Book III he knew that he was living in an age 'wherein the greatest part of men seem agreed to convert reading into an amusement, and to reject everything that requires any considerable degree of attention to be comprehended' (T, 456). This is not mere pique, but an accurate estimate of the climate of opinion.

He had done what he could in the *Abstract* to draw attention to the main themes of the *Treatise*. The *Treatise* suffered from its length and discursiveness; he tried in the *Abstract* to present a 'chain of reasoning, that is more simple and concise, where the chief propositions only are link't on to each other, illustrated by some simple examples, and confirmed by a few of the more forcible arguments', as he expresses his intention in the Preface. That venture, too, proved quite unsuccessful. No one, it appeared, was prepared to discuss his logic. So he turned to his main theme, Morals and Politics, but in a spirit chastened by his failures. However, he was still not quite reconciled to the failure of his logic to make any impression. In the first *Enquiry* he tried again, combining the technique of the *Abstract* with the 'sprightly style' he had been forging in his Moral and Political Essays. The sections on space and time disappeared because he intended to write another work on 'the metaphysical principles of geometry'² in which those sections would have found a natural home. In the *Enquiry* they

---

¹ *Essay*, Fourth Edition, pp. 430-71. In the seventh edition (p. 431) Beattie drops the word 'sprightly'.   ² *Letters*, II, 253.

would have interrupted the development of his main theme. The detailed analysis of perception goes with them. It had been a digression in the *Treatise*; Hume's youthful ardour had tempted him into discussions which were not really, so he now thought, essential to his main purpose. When, later, his critics insisted on devoting their attention to unessential points in the *Treatise*, ignoring the logic which Hume took to be its major achievement, he was irritated to the point of composing his famous disavowal of the *Treatise* as a juvenile work.[1]

The *Enquiry*, for all Hume's pains, was at first no more successful than his earlier work in arousing discussion of his logic although it did annoy the zealots. He had invited the judgment of his peers; no one had anything to say which would lead him to revise his opinions. Now he abandons philosophy, if by philosophy we mean the study of logic or metaphysics or epistemology for its own sake. But Hume had sought to show that philosophy was, in fact, reducible to the science of human nature; for him, politics, economics and history are still 'philosophy'. His original plan he at no time abandons; in that plan the content of Book I of the *Treatise* has only a preliminary and auxiliary role to play. In his political and economic writings, he regularly insists on points of a methodological kind; in the *Dialogues concerning Natural Religion* he expounds and develops his logic in opposition to theology; but he had 'completed' his logic, he thought, in the sense that its main principles were firmly established in the *Treatise*. Now the time had come to advance on that foundation.

[1] First published in the posthumous edition of 1777.

CHAPTER II

THE CRITIC OF FORMAL LOGIC

'THE sole end of logic', according to Hume, 'is to explain the principles and operations of our reasoning faculty, and the nature of our ideas' (T, xix). In this extended sense of the word, the whole of Book I of the *Treatise*—his discrimination between different kinds of perceptions no less than his theory of causal inference—forms part of Hume's logic. This is not, in itself, an innovation. The Port Royal logic, to take only one case, begins in a similar fashion, with 'reflections on ideas, or the first operation of the mind, which is called conceiving'. The 'idea' or, in Hume's language, the 'perception' is on this view the unit of reasoning; from it logic, as the 'theory of reasoning', must take its departure. At the same time, ideas are 'mental'. Thus the conventional doctrine already starts Hume along the road which is to lead him to the identification of logical with psychological problems. Logic and psychology have the same ingredients; Hume's distinction between impressions and ideas can therefore serve as the foundation both of his logic and of his psychology. It remains for him to show that the relations between the ingredients are also in both cases the same—that formal relations are nothing more than psychological links. Then it will follow that logic, in its entirety, forms part of the science of human nature.

Further comparison with the Port Royal logic brings to light the crucial difference between Hume's and the post-Cartesian logic. Logic is there defined as 'the art of directing reason aright for the instruction both of ourselves and others'. The intention is distinctly more pedagogic than Hume's; more important still, logic is restricted to *right* reasoning. This suggests a distinction between logic and psychology: logic is normative—it seeks to discover rules—whereas psychology merely *describes* the workings of the mind. The revolutionary character of Hume's logic consists in his rejection of this contrast; logic, he wishes to argue, is simply a branch of the descriptive moral sciences, being that part of them which is concerned with the understanding, as distinct from the passions. 'Right reasoning' has no legislative force; to describe it is not to formulate rules, but to show in what a certain kind of thinking consists—the sort we call 'scientific'.

Sometimes, indeed, Hume uses the word 'logic' in a more restricted sense, as when he says that his 'rules for judging of causes and effects' are 'all the logic' which he thinks 'proper to employ' (T, 175). At this point, like Descartes in the *Discourse on Method*, he is laying down rules which will serve as a substitute for the traditional rules of logic; naturally, therefore, he falls back into the conventional usage. These 'rules', as we shall see, are at once a necessity and an embarrassment to him. There is no room for them within a logic which is purely descriptive, and which admits no implication, but only inference.

This view about the nature of logic is the most important, and the most original, tendency in Hume's thinking. But we must make a distinction; there are, or are meant to be, *two* logics in Hume, the logic of Reason, and the logic of the Understanding. Reason demonstrates: its logic is the logic of necessary truths. At one stage, Hume suggests that even this sort of necessity can be reduced to a psychological fact: 'the necessity, which makes two times two equal to four, or three angles of a triangle equal to two right ones, lies only in the act of the understanding, by which we consider and compare these ideas' (T, 166). But the general tenor of his argument is that demonstrated propositions have an objective necessity, which can be contrasted with the merely subjective, or 'internal', necessity of causal relations. The understanding cannot demonstrate; causal inference is its method; and causal inference never leads us to necessary truths but only to 'matters of fact'. Our inference is a fact; it is a fact, and one we can further investigate, that our mind develops habits of expectation. But that investigation does not reveal any 'necessary connexion' between what we expect and what has already happened. From this, Hume thinks, it follows that there is no logical foundation for, as distinct from psychological description of, our causal inferences: an objective

logic, it is tacitly assumed, must be a logic of 'necessary connexions'.

If, then, formal logic has anywhere a province, it will be as
the logic of Reason, the theory of demonstration, and demonstration, so Hume argues, is never possible except in
mathematics. Locke had excepted morals as well as mathematics. The proposition 'where there is no property, there is
no injustice' is, he wrote, 'as certain as anything in Euclid'.
His supporting argument runs thus: 'the idea of property
being a right to anything, and the idea to which the name
"injustice" is given being the invasion or violation of that right;
it is evident that these ideas being thus established, and these
names annexed to them, I can as certainly know this proposition to be true as that a triangle has three angles equal to two
right ones'.[1] Hume needed no great perspicacity to see that
'this proposition is nothing but a more imperfect definition';
and the same is true, he concludes, of 'all those pretended
syllogistic reasonings, which may be found in every other
branch of learning, except the sciences of quantity and number'
(E, 163). This, it should be noted, is a very great step from
saying that *demonstration* is peculiar to mathematics. It is one
thing to say that only in mathematics can there be formally
valid reasoning from necessarily true premises (demonstration);
it is quite another thing, and much less plausible, to argue that
formally valid reasoning ('syllogistic reasonings') has nowhere
else any force. Yet Hume makes the transition (he is, of course,
not alone in so doing) without apparently observing that there
is one. A 'deductive logic', it is assumed, demands self-
evident premises; if the premises are 'probable', then, equally,
the connexion between premises and conclusion must be
probable—or, in its modern sense, 'inductive'. And probable
connexions, it is then argued, are non-implicative.

The case of mathematics, then, is supposed to be unique; here
alone is there demonstration, and only where there is demonstration can there be objective, formal implication. Even this
exception is an awkward one; Hume's theory of ideas leaves
no room for mathematical demonstration. He takes over, and

[1] *Essay*, IV, iii, 18.

develops in his own way, Malebranche's doctrine that 'les jugements, les raisonnements simples et les raisonnements composés ne sont que de pures perceptions de la part de l'entendement, parce que l'entendement ne fait simplement qu'apercevoir'.[1]

It is 'a very remarkable error', Hume considers, to divide 'acts of the understanding' into 'conception, judgment and reasoning'. All these acts 'resolve themselves into the first, and are nothing but particular ways of conceiving our objects' (T, 97n). In each case, we are confronted by an idea; judgment does not involve the uniting of ideas, or reasoning the interposition of a third idea.

Although it appears in a footnote, this conflation is of great importance to Hume. It enables him to regard 'X exists' as a judgment, although it contains, on his view, no more than the single idea 'X'; more important still, it enables him to define a belief as a 'vivid idea', a definition which is obviously defective unless 'ideas' includes 'judgments'. And most important of all, it is essential to Hume's account of causal reasoning. That reasoning consists in the discovery of intermediate ideas was a point on which Locke and the Port Royal logicians could agree;[2] the number of ideas involved was the criterion by which 'ideas' were distinguished from 'judgments' and 'judgments' from 'inferences'. Locke might criticize the syllogism, but he still maintained, although only at a relatively late stage in the composition of the *Essay*,[3] that demonstration involves mediation, as distinct from direct intuition. This theory of reasoning would cut across Hume's account of causal inference. In causal inference 'we infer a cause immediately from its effect'; there are, then, only two ideas involved, with no third,

---

[1] *Recherche*, VI, I, 2 (Vol. II, p. 262).

[2] *Essay*, IV, xvii, 4; *Port Royal Logic*, Part III, Ch. i.

[3] cf. L. Roth, *Descartes' Discourse on Method*, p. 114 ff. Roth points out that in the early drafts of Locke's essay demonstration is 'intuition'—seeing that a proposition must be true—and that it is only in the final version of the *Essay* that Locke accepts the Cartesian doctrine of mediation. He suggests further that Locke's reflection on the Cartesian theory of mathematics was what led him in this direction. Locke, on this interpretation, saw the difficulties, of which Hume remained unconscious, in Malebranche's theory of knowledge as 'vision'.

mediating, idea. 'And this inference', he continues, 'is not only a true species of reasoning, but the strongest of all others, and more convincing than when we interpose another idea to connect the two extremes' (T, 97n). Inference, therefore, cannot be defined as involving mediation; and 'interposing another idea' is only a matter of extending the range of one's vision.

Hume can in this way avoid one of the leading awkwardnesses in Locke's theory. Locke begins by defining an idea as 'whatsoever is the object of the understanding when a man thinks', but ends by arguing that our knowledge is not of ideas, but of 'relations of agreement', in which our ideas are only constituents. If, as Hume maintains, 'whether we consider a single object or several', it is still the case that 'the act of mind exceeds not a single conception', then Locke's inconsistent distinction between ideas, knowledge and demonstration will disappear; the unit of knowledge is the idea, into which both knowledge and demonstration are absorbed.

But a new difficulty arises. If mathematicians never made mistakes, and if proofs presented no difficulty to them, it might be plausible to argue that mathematical 'arguments' are simply conceptions. That mathematicians err, however, is a fact of which any theory has to give some account; this is what forces Descartes to distinguish, however half-heartedly, between 'intuition' and demonstration, and Hume, in the same way, is led to contrast 'rules' with 'their application', as if 'application'—deduction—were quite distinct from simple conception. In the *Enquiry*, furthermore, we find him admitting that demonstration 'by a variety of mediums' is essential to 'the sciences of quantity and number' (E, 163); as we have already seen, he is prepared to defend, in those sciences, the use of syllogism. Here, at least, Hume has to adopt the traditional logic, however disturbing it might be to the consistency of his general theory. Ideas are what they are known as being; a mathematical demonstration is an idea—the conclusion ought to be that any such demonstration is what it is known as being, and hence that mathematical errors are impossible. Hume naturally boggles at this consequence; but the effect is that the objective implication of mathematics persists as an undigested residue in his logical system. When mathematics is the theme, he constantly relapses into the 'remarkable errors' of the traditional logicians.

So much for the logic of Reason: here is an exception to Hume's general scheme, but one he feels he can pass over as not being of any great consequence; it is, on the other hand, vital for him to show that the logic of the understanding, the logic of empirical science, involves no formal connexions but only psychological links. But it will be best first to pause at the point at which Hume's two logics come together, his theory of philosophical relations. We shall see very clearly displayed the indirect way in which Hume makes essential formal distinctions, distinctions which he is intent on not making directly, just on account of their irreducibility to the merely psychological.

The theory of philosophical relations is another Lockian episode: it is presumed, as in the case of mathematics, that having ideas is one thing, comparing them quite another. Locke had written: 'there could be no room for any positive knowledge at all, if we could not perceive any relation between our ideas, and find out the agreement or disagreement they have one with another, in several ways the mind takes of comparing them'.[1] Hume accepted this conclusion, but was not satisfied with Locke's list of 'agreements' and transforms it into something like a theory of categories, in Kant's sense of the word. He calls the relations 'philosophical' not because they have anything in particular to do with philosophy, but on the ground that the 'natural' use of relation confines it to things which are linked closely together; no one but a philosopher, the suggestion is, would describe 'a thousand miles apart' as signifying a relation. At the same time these relations are certainly distinguished from one another with an eye to the philosophy which is to follow, and Hume's brief and apparently casual discussion raises a multitude of philosophical problems.

All relations, Hume argues,[2] involve resemblance, since 'no objects will admit of comparison, but what have some degree of resemblance'. 'Resemblance' is Hume's substitute for Locke's

[1] *Essay*, IV, i, 5.　[2] Except where otherwise indicated, all quotations in the discussion which follows are from Book I, Part 1, § 5 of the *Treatise*.

'agreement', and, in part, for 'disagreement' as well. At the same time, 'resemblance' is the name of a quite specific relation, which plays a very important role in Hume's psychology. Herein lies a major difficulty: resemblance is at once a specific relation and that which underlies every relation. We are again reminded of Locke, in whose philosophy 'agreement' functions in an equally ambiguous way, for it is, on the face of it, a particular species of relation, and yet every relation is supposed to be a species of agreement.

This ambiguity arises, I suggest, because both Hume and Locke are trying to find a non-formal method of characterizing logical form. In Locke, as in Hume, there are two logics: in his case, the logic of necessary connexion, which is the logic of the real but inaccessible world, and the logic of co-existence, the logic to which the weakness of our faculties, if we except the special case of mathematics and morals, inevitably restricts us. Could we penetrate to the nature of things, we should see that A must be B; as matters stand, we can know only that our idea of A and our idea of B 'go together' or 'agree'. The traditional logic distinguished subject (as substance) from predicate (as attribute). On Locke's logic there can be no such distinction, for 'agreeing' is a symmetrical relation, and it holds between ideas which are all of the same ontological status. The distinction between subject and predicate is insignificant, grammatical merely, and so the form of the proposition must reside in some general relation (agreement or disagreement) between the constituent ideas; different forms will be describable as different types of agreement or disagreement.

Resemblance, similarly, is Hume's name for that which makes propositions possible, the 'comparability' of ideas in virtue of which they can stand as terms in propositions. He is attempting to give an account of logical form by making use of the obviously empirical relation of resemblance. But 'resemblance', thus understood, must be very different from resemblance in the sense in which we say 'Doesn't John resemble his father!', the sense in which resemblance, according to Hume, operates as an associative relation. No one, asked to defend the view that John resembled his father, would reply that John and his father both live a thousand miles away from Smith, nor even that they both have a spatio-temporal location. Hume is partly conscious of this difficulty. He shows symptoms of alarm, as resemblance, in its logical sense, threatens to undermine resemblance, in its associative sense. 'Tho' resemblance be necessary to all philosophical relation, it does not follow, that it always produces an association of ideas'; for, if it did, then, since all ideas resemble, in the sense of being comparable in some respect, resemblance could never explain why idea B rather than idea C follows idea A. Hume tries to overcome his difficulty thus: 'when a quality becomes very general, and is common to a great many individuals, it leads not the mind directly to any one of them'. Some types of resemblance, the argument would be, are so common that they do not act as an associative principle between ideas. The point is obscurely made, and Hume could not give any clear account of the distinction between 'very general' and 'less general' properties; but if he were to express the matter more precisely, by distinguishing between a formal and non-formal sense of resemblance, this would leave him with a formal logic on his hands, a contingency he is most anxious to avoid.

Hume's account of negation illustrates still more clearly his subterranean way of making formal distinctions. Locke had tried to give an account of the traditional distinction between affirmation and negation in terms of agreement and disagreement, with the curious consequence, as we have seen, that agreement and disagreement have to be regarded as 'highest kinds', every other relation, even the notion of relation itself, being a species of one or the other—although, very obviously, agreement and disagreement are themselves quite specific relations. Hume has now reduced affirmation to a specific relation, the relation of resemblance; the question is whether the same can be done for negation.

In part, Hume dismisses negation as the simple absence of relation. 'It might naturally be expected that I should join *difference* to the other relations. But that I consider rather as a negation of relation, than as anything real or positive.' Clearly, this doctrine is a quite unsatisfactory one; when we describe A as being unlike B (this constituting what Hume calls a difference in kind, as distinct from a numerical difference) we are comparing them just as much as when we draw attention to their resemblance: 'A is different from B' is as much a proposition as 'A is very like B'. Yet it is certainly an uncomfortable doctrine that 'unlikeness' is a species of resemblance; at this point, particularly, the empirical sense of resemblance cuts across the attempt to substitute it for the formal notion of propositional connexion. Negation is a logical constant of which the most desperately non-formal logic must give an account; and to say that 'is not' means 'is not related to' is certainly to burke the problem.

For the rest, negation appears as a constituent in what Hume calls 'contrariety', which is Hume's attempt to define the formal relations of contradiction and contrariety as a mode of comparison between ideas. Contrariety is not itself an associative relation, but it is supposed to be a combination of two such relations—Causation and Resemblance (E, 24n). Hence if the logical relations of contrariety and contradiction can be reduced to a relation of contrariety between ideas, yet another formal relationship will fit within the framework of associative theory, the study of it thus falling within the province of the science of mind. What he says about contrariety is, at first sight, singular in the extreme. 'Let us consider, that no ideas are in themselves contrary, except those of existence and non-existence.' Yet Hume steadily maintains that there is no idea of existence, and what an 'idea of non-existence' could be, not even his ingenuity could make out. But note the sequel: 'which ideas are plainly resembling, as implying both of them an idea of the object: tho' the latter excludes the object from all times and places, in which it is supposed not to exist.' To assert the non-existence of anything, it now appears, is to say that it does not occur at certain places and times; to assert its existence is to say that it does occur at those places and times. This is very different from Hume's official doctrine about existence-propositions, but it is not unparalleled in other places in which Hume is forced to discuss logical issues. 'The non-existence of any being', he writes, 'is as clear and distinct an idea as its existence' (E, 164). At this point in the *Enquiry* he is insisting that 'no negation of a fact can involve a contradiction'; every proposition, that is, has an intelligible contradictory. Now, if we cannot think of a thing except as existing, as Hume had previously argued, then we obviously cannot think of it as non-existent; and to contemplate 'the negation of a fact' would involve thinking simultaneously of an idea as existing (the fact) and as non-existing (the negation).

Hume's original doctrine, in fact, leaves him open to the Eleatic criticism of 'not-being'. If to think of anything is to think of it as existing, it follows that 'not-being' can never be thought of. But if 'not-being' refers to the non-existence of a certain quality *in a certain place and time*, then we can talk about 'not-being' without being obliged to contemplate an idea as both existing and not-existing. And this is the interpretation of 'non-existence'—with the correlative interpretation of 'existence'—on which Hume must fall back in order to give any account of contradiction. In other words, he is obliged to think of 'contrariety' as holding between propositions, not between ideas as such. He can describe it as 'involving resemblance' because these propositions 'resemble', in as far as it is the same quality which they assert or deny to exist in a certain place. Their terms (or 'variables') are identical; it is their formal properties ('logical constants') which differ.

The obscurity of Hume's theory of contrariety derives from his attempt, in the interests of a logic in which the only links are psychological, to avoid this contrast between formal and non-formal, a contrast which is also implicit in his description of existence and non-existence as the only 'ideas' which are 'in themselves contrary'. This is an obscure way of saying that 'X is Y' and 'X is not Y' are the only propositions which are *formally* incompatible; to see their incompatibility we do not need any special knowledge of 'X' or 'Y'. 'All other objects', by contrast, 'such as fire and water, heat, and cold, are only found to be contrary from experience, and from the contrariety of their causes or effects.' These 'objects' are the 'opposites' of the *Phaedo*; Hume is suggesting that their contrariety consists in the causal fact that one drives the other out. To know that 'X is fiery' and 'X is watery' are incompatible is to have the special knowledge about fire and water that water quenches fire. This sort of contrariety Hume's causal interpretation of 'matter of fact' propositions can hope to compass; causal relations are expressible in psychological terms; it is *formal* contrariety which compels him to depart so violently from his general presumptions. More generally, he cannot account for affirmation and negation; these are not relations parallel to 'greater than' or 'distant from': they are needed for each of these relations (*is* or *is not* greater than) but are themselves significant quite independently of all such relations; they are fundamental in a sense which Hume, beginning as he does from 'perceptions' as distinct from propositions and intent as he is on destroying all *formal* logic, has not the slightest hope of explaining.

Furthermore, the attempted reduction of 'X is Y' to 'X and Y resemble' is, on the face of it, a quite misleading account of the meaning of most ordinary propositions. Hume makes more plausible his emphasis on resemblance—an emphasis important for his associationist scheme—by constantly choosing mathematical examples. It was already a familiar view that mathematical propositions assert the partial or total congruity of their terms—a view which Hume re-formulates by saying that they assert the numerical resemblance of the ideas which compose them. Geometry is imperfect; for we have no precise way of determining how many points a line contains; we must be content, in that case, with close resemblance between the lines or figures we are comparing (T, 45). In algebra and arithmetic the units are precise; in this case, resemblance appears in the form of exact equality.

But whatever may be said about mathematical propositions, Hume could scarcely maintain that a proposition like 'gold is yellow', for example, means the same as 'our idea of gold and our idea of yellow resemble one another'; iron pyrites resembles gold, but it would be an error to say that it *is* gold: 'resembling X' and 'being X' are quite distinct notions. How then are such propositions as these to be fitted within the framework of associative connexions? The answer must be that such propositions are ways of asserting spatial and temporal contiguities—what Locke calls 'going together' and Hume 'situations in time and place' (T, 73). This was really the outcome of Locke's analysis of empirical knowledge, a fact which is somewhat obscured by his illicit reference beyond ideas to substances and real essences. No other analysis is possible if all our knowledge is of perceptions; matter-of-fact propositions must relate them in temporal and spatial sequences and co-existences. (That is why Hume's elaborate discussion on space and time precedes his analysis of empirical knowledge.)

But Hume does not rest at this point; it is only a stepping-stone (and not a clearly delineated one) to his analysis of the logic of the understanding. Propositions which assert anything more than the present situation of an object, he wishes to show, must all of them rest upon causal reasoning. Provided we are content to say that 'this X is near that Y', no reasoning is involved; for we restrict our judgment to what lies immediately before our senses. But as soon as we assert that 'whenever X is, Y is' (all X are Y), we are committing ourself to a belief about entities we are not actually observing; and any such belief must be the consequence of causal reasonings. 'There is nothing in any objects to perswade us', he says, 'that they are either always *remote* or always *contiguous*; and when from experience and observation we discover that their relation in this particular is invariable, we always conclude there is some secret *cause*, which separates or unites them' (T, 74). And, as he expresses the matter in the *Enquiry*, 'on this [the causal relation] are founded all our reasonings concerning matter of fact or existence' (E, 76). Every 'belief', every empirical proposition except those which are the objects of direct perception, or at least every *rational* belief—on this crucial point Hume vacillates —arises out of a causal inference.

Yet according to Hume a cause is always an efficient cause, a prior condition. 'All causes', he explicitly argues, 'are of the same kind', and 'there is no foundation for that distinction, which we sometimes make between efficient causes and causes *sine qua non*; or between efficient causes, and formal, and material, and exemplary, and final causes' (T, 171). At this stage, a cause is officially defined as 'an object precedent and contiguous to another, and where all the objects resembling the former are plac'd in like relations of precedence and contiguity to those objects, that resemble the latter' (T, 170). Spatial contiguity eventually fades away, but priority remains; Hume's minimal definition is expressed in the *Enquiry*: 'an object, followed by another, and where all the objects similar to the first are followed by objects similar to the second' (E, 76).

Now take the case where A *always* goes with B. How, on this definition of 'cause', can Hume intelligibly speak of such universal contiguities as having a cause? Just because the contiguity of A and B is universal, there is nothing prior to it. Thus, if, to take an example which Hume uses in a different connexion, a certain taste and a certain smell are constantly contiguous, it is surely meaningless to ask for the efficient cause of this contiguity: there could be such a cause only if at one time the taste and smell were not together, in which case we could ask what brought them together. Similarly, it is meaningless to talk, as Hume does, of 'the *cause* of attraction' (T, 13). In his sense of the word 'caused', it is unintelligible to speak of attraction as 'caused'; it could have a cause only if at one time bodies did not attract one another—in which case the laws of attraction would no longer be universal.

What Hume is trying to do is to subsume every case of explanation, or 'giving a reason', under the head of causal inference. He feels confident that he can show that inference of this sort does not rest upon any sort of implicative relation, and, more positively, that it does rest upon a trick of the mind, which it is for psychology to describe. If when we give a reason we are always engaging in a causal inference, it will follow that reasoning is a process which is describable in wholly psychological terms, not as the discovery of implications, but as the habit of thinking in certain ways. But Hume does not succeed in showing that all inference is in fact causal.

He is forced, again and again, to point to implicative relations outside the field of mathematics, and thus to admit that there are necessary connexions between propositions which are not necessary truths. Take the case of 'general rules', which come to play an increasingly prominent part in Hume's philosophy. He tries to argue that they arise out of our experience of constant conjunction, and that to employ them, therefore, is to make use of causal inference, although in an 'oblique' manner. But, whatever the origin of these rules, the fact remains that the inferences by means of which we apply them to particular cases are certainly not causal inferences. One of the most important of these general rules is that 'like objects placed in like circumstances will always produce like effects'. Hume invokes this principle in order to overcome an acute difficulty in his theory of causal inference. According to his general theory, we say that A is the cause of B when our experience of the constant priority of A to B has produced in us the habit of expecting B when we encounter A. But he feels constrained to admit that a single experience of A as prior to B is sometimes sufficient; we conclude immediately that A is the cause of B. 'This difficulty will vanish', he suggests, 'if we consider, that tho' we are here supposed to have had only one experiment of a particular effect, yet we have many millions to convince us of this principle: that like objects, plac'd in like circumstances, will always produce like effects' (T, 105). This principle being firmly established, it bestows an equal firmness 'on any opinion to which it can be *apply'd*'; the particular case is 'comprehended' under the general principle. But this 'application', this 'comprehension', must surely be some sort of formally valid reasoning. Even if, as Hume argues, the constant conjunctions we experience can generate in us a belief in a principle, as distinct from a simple habit of expectation, the fact remains that in using the principle we rely upon a formal implication. We have come to believe a matter of fact—that A causes B— by the help of a general principle, by arguing that since like causes like, what is like A will cause what is like B; the principle certainly does not *cause* the case to which it is applied. Yet without the help of this general rule—and there are others of no less importance—he cannot even pretend to give an account of the genesis of our ordinary beliefs.

This defect is even more conspicuous in Hume's theory of testimony. Only causal inference, Hume argues, 'informs us of existences and objects, which we do not see or feel' (T, 74); it alone can enable us to infer that something has occurred, or will occur, which we did not actually perceive. And this is, to Hume, the great importance of causal inference, that it carries us beyond the narrow range of immediate sensory experience. Yet Hume has also argued that causal inference consists simply in this: that having in the past experienced A as constantly prior to B, we are led to expect B on experiencing A. From this definition T. H. Green concludes that 'the inferred idea can be no new one, but must itself be an idea of memory, and the question, how any one's knowledge comes to extend beyond the range of his memory, remains unanswered'.[1] Other commentators are more kindly disposed. Hendel, for example, argues that 'no inference is mere recall . . . it is essentially the conception of some object *similar* to the one now present to us . . . inference is imaginative'.[2] But Green is clearly right: we can be led to expect only what we have previously experienced; if we depart from that experience—so far as it is possible to do so—we are not inferring, we are indulging in a flight of fancy. Such fancies form no part of the 'real world', no part of what Hume calls 'the system of the judgment' (T, 108). Even on the most favourable interpretation, from the present point of view, the most experience can teach us to expect is that something *very like* what we have previously experienced will come to pass; it can never lead us to infer the existence of a genuinely novel entity.

How could Hume imagine otherwise? Only because 'testimony' is illicitly subsumed under the general head of 'causal' inference, as becomes especially clear in the tenth chapter of the *Enquiry*, *Of Miracles*. The argument of that chapter, it must be remembered, was originally meant to form part of the *Treatise*; and without it the *Treatise* is incomplete. When we consider the reasoning of that book in its present form, it seems quite ridiculous for Hume to write that 'by means of it [causal inference] I paint the Universe in my imagination, and fix my attention

[1] Introduction to Hume's *Treatise*, § 331.   [2] *Studies*, p. 186.

on any part of it I please. I form an idea of Rome, which I neither see nor remember; but which is connected with such impressions as I remember to have received from the conversation and books of travellers' (T, 108). We naturally object that our experience reveals no constant conjunction between impressions of books and impressions of Rome. *Of Miracles* at least attempts to answer this objection. 'Our assurance of any argument of this kind is derived from no other principle than our observation of the veracity of human testimony, and of the usual conformity of facts to the reports of witnesses. It being a general maxim, that no objects have any discoverable connexion together, and that all the inferences, which we can draw from one to another, are founded merely on our experience of their constant and regular conjunction; it is evident, that we ought not to make an exception to this maxim in favour of human testimony, whose connexion with any event seems, in itself, as little necessary as any other' (E, 111).

Yet there are symptoms of uneasiness. 'This species of reasoning, perhaps, one may deny to be founded on the relation of cause and effect'. The reply is immediate—'I shall not dispute about a word'—and then follows the argument we have quoted above. 'Not dispute about a word'—not even when, like 'cause', it has been so carefully and so often defined both in the *Treatise* and in the *Enquiry*! It is not 'words' which are in question; the real issue is whether all inference fits into the pattern Hume has laid down. Argument from testimony runs thus: 'A witness W asserts p, ∴ p is true'. As Hume points out, this inference rests on 'the general rule' that whatever is asserted by witnesses of the type T (to which W belongs) is always true. And no doubt, as he argues, this rule derives from 'experience'. But although it sometimes happens that we first experience an event and then later listen to a true account of it, in many other cases we meet first with the testimony and only later with the event. And very often we experience the testimony but not the event, or an event without any testimony. On Hume's theory of causality, then, it is impossible to regard the event as the cause of the testimony or the testimony as the cause of the event; the sequence of impressions is a highly irregular one. Furthermore, even if the 'general rule' could be causally derived, the fact remains that the inference from the rule to a particular case—from 'witnesses of the type T are reliable' to 'W is reliable'—is certainly not a causal inference; and it points to a formal implication.

To sum up, Hume does not succeed in showing that formal reasoning can be restricted to the special case of mathematics, or that all deductive reasoning in the empirical sciences can be reduced to non-implicative causal inference. His errors are instructive. He was not the last to believe that unless the premises in an argument are 'necessary truths', the argument itself must be non-deductive. Nor was he the last to lay such overwhelming stress on the importance of efficient causality in empirical science. His account of testimony is obviously inadequate; but this is merely a particular illustration of a more general weakness. He cannot consistently maintain that every rationally held belief derives from our experience of causal conjunctions. Experience comes to mean 'constant conjunction' without any reference to the specifically causal factor of priority. Yet his official doctrine is still that *causal* conjunction must be the source of all empirical inference.

Why is he so anxious to insist on this point? One main reason is that inferences like 'All X are Y, this is X and therefore this is Y' cannot be plausibly reduced to a trick of the mind, or supposed to consist in a mere habit of expectation. Inferences of the form 'X has been, and therefore Y will be' can with much more plausibility be so interpreted. And unless inferences are nothing but habits of the mind, the doctrine of the priority of the mind is threatened; there will be objective interconnexions, of which Man is not the measure.

Nor was there anything revolutionary, anything to provoke resistance, in this emphasis on causality. It seemed to follow, naturally enough, from the arguments of his empiricist predecessors. He did not have to construct it *ab initio* for his science of man; he found it (substantially) already in existence. Empiricists have always been inclined to believe that science is the discovery of causal connexions; to take only one case, that had been Hobbes' view. 'Philosophy', says Hobbes, 'is such knowledge of effects and appearances, as we acquire by true ratiocination from the knowledge we have first of their causes or generation; and again of such causes and generations as may be from knowing first their effects'.[1] Hobbes, it is important to notice, thought that 'the end of knowledge is power'; and Hume writes, in a similar vein, that 'the only immediate utility of all sciences, is to teach us how to control, and regulate future events by their causes' (E, 76). It is first presumed that science seeks to control, and then concluded that, since we can only control the future, science must be a method of prediction; it supplies us with a rational substitute for soothsaying. It is the practicality of empiricists, I suggest, which has led them so much to exaggerate the importance of causality for science.

Furthermore, this emphasis on causality accords with the atomistic particularism which Locke and Berkeley bequeathed to Hume. A cause is one perception; an effect is a quite different perception; perceptions can be causally connected, so Hume was to argue, while still remaining 'loose and separate', in the sense that each *could* be different without the other being different. A cause is a particular event, occurring here and now, or there and then; the emphasis is where Hume wanted it to be, on the particularity of our experience. If, on the other hand, science relates propositions one to another, there is already connexion within the proposition; if it were different, any propositions which imply it must also be different; and at least the predicate in every proposition is obviously a general term. Science, to Hume, *imposes* connexions; it does not *discover* them (with the exception of spatial and temporal order, which Hume describes as a conjunction, as distinct from a connexion); this is to be the source of his scepticism and to justify his emphasis on the science of man. And this, above all, is the doctrine which his analysis of causality is meant to illustrate.

To turn now to that analysis: Hume must first show that implication (understood as 'demonstration') plays no part in causal reasoning. In the first place, the cause does not *imply* the effect. The view he is rejecting has been clearly formulated by G. F. Stout: 'A cause is such a reason, so that if we had a

---

[1] *De Corpore*, English translation ed. Molesworth (*Works*, Vol. 1, p. 3).

sufficiently comprehensive knowledge of what really takes place, we should see how and why the effect follows from the cause with logical necessity.'[1] However 'comprehensive' our knowledge of the cause, Hume argued, we can never observe any necessity in the relation of cause to effect. Sometimes, indeed, he speaks with the Lockians; he is content to insist that 'the ultimate causes are unknown to us', that 'no philosopher, who is rational or modest, has ever pretended to assign the ultimate cause of any natural operation, or to show distinctly the action of that power, which produces any single effect in the universe' (E, 30). His main anxiety is to show that experience reveals to us no necessary connexion between cause and effect; if anyone likes to believe that such necessary connexions none the less exist, beyond the range of any possible experience, Hume will let him indulge his fancy.

A general theory of necessity is presumed: if A is necessarily connected with B, then from our knowledge of A alone we ought to be able to deduce the existence of B. And this we cannot do. 'There is no object, which implies the existence of any other' (T, 86); 'let an object be presented to a man of ever so strong natural reason and abilities; if that object be entirely new to him, he will not be able, by the most accurate examination of its sensible qualities, to discover any of its causes or effects' (E, 27). Sometimes the argument is formulated in the manner of a rationalist. If causes imply their effects, then causal inference 'would amount to knowledge, and wou'd imply the absolute contradiction and impossibility of conceiving anything different'. 'But', he continues, 'since all distinct ideas are separable, 'tis evident there can be no impossibility of that kind' (T, 87). It is always conceivable that X should produce Z rather than Y; hence X does not imply Y. The criterion of conceivability, however, is not essential to his argument: it is enough to appeal to experience. Given that this is X, no scientific enquiry could show us, prior to experience, that it will produce Y; to discover its effects, we must watch X in action.

[1] 'Mechanical and Teleological Causality', *Proc. Ar. Soc.*, Supp., Vol. XXIV, p. 1. See also *Mind and Matter* (*passim*) and *God and Nature*, with my memoir in the latter volume.

If the causal relation is not implication, how is it to be characterized? When we look at a single causal relation, Hume argues, we observe nothing more than this: that the cause is prior and contiguous to the effect. But, he continues, we do not describe one thing as the cause of another simply because the first is *on one occasion* contiguous and prior to the second; we require that they be *constantly* conjoined. Constant conjunction settles the matter. 'We remember to have seen that species of object we call flame, and to have felt that species of sensation we call heat. We likewise call to mind their constant conjunction in all past instances. Without any farther ceremony, we call the one *cause* and the other *effect*, and infer the existence of the one from that of the other' (T, 87). The problem now is to discover the ground of that inference. Our experience is that A and B were constantly conjoined in the past; how does this entitle us to conclude that the A we are *now* experiencing will be followed by a B we have never previously experienced?

Obviously, we cannot argue that since A *always has been* conjoined with B, therefore it *must always be* so conjoined. At least we can so argue, and do so argue, but the inference, on Hume's view, is not 'a chain of reasoning', is not demonstrative. 'I shall allow, if you please, that the one proposition may justly be inferred from the other; I know, in fact, that it always is inferred. But if you insist that the inference is made by a chain of reasoning, I desire you to produce that reasoning' (E, 34). Past conjunction does not immediately imply future conjunction; reasoning from past to future, if it is to be formally valid, will have to make use of some principle connecting past with future cases. Such a principle is suggested in the *Treatise*: 'instances of which we have had no experience, must resemble those of which we have had experience' or, as he also puts it, 'the course of nature continues always uniformly the same' (T, 89). If causal reasoning is demonstrative, then, Hume argues, the opposite of this principle of uniformity must be inconceivable. But 'we can easily conceive a' change in the course of nature'; hence the argument is not a demonstration. Nor can we, without circularity, assert that the reasoning is at least 'probable', for unless we know independently that causal reasoning is valid, we cannot distinguish 'probable reasoning', resting as it does on causal inference, from mere idle speculation.

Hume's argument at this point is somewhat odd. For although we can conceive a change in the course of nature, if this means only that we can think of a particular thing as behaving in a way in which it does not now behave, we certainly cannot conceive a change of such character that future *instances* in no way resemble past *instances*. In these circumstances, they would not be ' instances'. Here, as elsewhere, the vague reference to resemblance' obscures logical issues. The principle we should need is not that future instances must have some resemblance to past instances (which is a tautology) but that if a thing has behaved in a certain way in the past, it must always behave in that same way in the future; and this principle is not only undemonstrable but actually false.

There is, in fact, no possible way of 'justifying' an inference from 'X is *sometimes* conjoined with Y' to 'X is *always* conjoined with Y', if 'justifying' means finding a proposition such that with its help the second of these propositions would follow from the first. If, then, 'constantly conjoined in our experience' simply means 'conjoined in some cases, viz. those we happen to have experienced', Hume's argument is irrefutable; we are never 'justified' (in its logical sense) in asserting that A is invariably conjoined with B.

But we can go further than this: on Hume's general assumptions we are not even entitled to say that A has been constantly conjoined with B in our experience; and if we are entitled to say this, we are equally entitled to say that it is *always* conjoined with B. If it be really true, as Hume sometimes asserts, that we experience the species A conjoined with the species B, then our experience from the beginning is of the A-kind of thing conjoined with the B-kind of thing, and the distinction of instances into 'past' and 'future' is quite irrelevant.

We can observe directly that an A-thing is a B-thing; we need no 'constant conjunction' to assure us that our universal propositions are true; and our fear of the future will be no greater than our fear of the present. We shall be well aware that our observations may be erroneous. Perhaps it will turn out that only a certain kind of A-thing is a B-thing. But equally we might be wrong in supposing that what now confronts us is an A-thing. Things behave in unexpected ways, not only in the future but *now*. It is no more difficult to be sure that all men are mortal than it is to be sure that Jones is dead. Hume's problem would then be transformed; constant conjunction would lose the importance he ascribes to it, and his problem would be converted into a more general one—how do we know that any empirical proposition is true?—a problem which, just because it is so generalized, looks much less alarming than the classical problem of induction.

Hume's references to our experience of species, however, might be set down to his speaking with the vulgar; his general view is certainly that our experience is of particulars. Yet clearly he cannot say that our experience is of *purely* specific cases. For then constant conjunction would vanish. Our experience would be of *this thus with that*. Each conjunction would be as unique as the events it conjoins.

In his official definitions of causality, therefore, Hume writes as a nominalist, neither of the repetition of instances nor of the conjunction of species, but of the conjunction of 'like objects', linked to other present objects by contiguity and to past objects by resemblance.

But if 'resemblance' means 'belonging to the same species', or 'having properties in common', then we are back where we were; our experience is of general connexions. If, on the other hand, it means 'having qualities rather like one another', then (even if this analysis is intelligible) there is no constant conjunction to provoke in us a habit of expectation. There will be sequences, A-B, C-D, E-F, in which A, C, E are rather alike, but the occurrence of a G also rather like A, C, E cannot provoke us to have a vivid idea of B rather than of D or F; and there is no way in which it could lead us to anticipate the quite distinct perception H. If conjunction is to form habits, it must really be *constant*; but if it is constant, then we do not experience unique occurrences: our experience, from the beginning, must be of kinds of things. (Of course, it does not follow that we shall always *recognize* that they are of this kind or of that kind; our reactions will often be habitual, as Hume suggests. There is an ambiguity in ' our experience is of kinds of things' which can easily mislead us into interpreting all habitual reactions as the discovery of universal propositions—every 'knowing how' as a 'knowing that'—an error the reverse of Hume's.)

That we are directly acquainted with generality is a possibility which Hume never contemplates, not surprisingly, in view of the unanimity of his contemporaries. As Berkeley had expressed the matter: 'It is a universal maxim that everything which exists is particular.'[1] And 'particular' must here be interpreted in a sense which, by a species of 'vicious intellectualism', prevents things from being also universal. If, in Hobbes' succinct phrase, 'experience concludeth nothing universally', if all we can ever learn from experience is that X is *sometimes* Y, then Hume is quite right in concluding that no 'principle' could ever bridge the gap between the particular propositions with which experience presents us and the universal propositions which we none the less believe to be true. But, in fact, if we take seriously the doctrine that experience knows nothing of generality, then it is as impossible to observe that X is now Y, or is sometimes Y, or always has been Y, as that it always will be Y; the generality of X and Y is no more, or no less, a matter of experience than the universality of their connexion.[2] (The notorious inadequacy of Hume's theory of abstract ideas—and Berkeley's—derives from this very difficulty.) In this respect, the problem was misleadingly stated for Hume's successors; as if there were no difficulty in our knowing that Socrates is dead, but a problem if we wish to assert that all men are mortal.

Hume is now satisfied. He has made his point: a cause does not imply its effect directly, and there is no general principle with the help of which we can deduce from our experience that one thing is the cause of another. If we are asked for our

[1] 'First Dialogue Between Hylas and Philonous' (*Works*, ed. Fraser, Vol. I, p. 403).

[2] As I have tried to show in some detail in my articles on 'Logical Positivism', more especially the first of them (*Austr. Jnl. of Psych. and Phil.*, Vol. XXI, p. 65). See also John Anderson, 'Empiricism' (*ibid.* Vol. v, p. 241) and 'The Problem of Causality' (*ibid.*, Vol. x, p. 81).

evidence that A is the cause of B, the only possible answer, he considers, is that A and B have been constantly conjoined in the past, and this does nothing to *prove* that they are invariably associated one with another. Since all empirical inference is causal, it follows that outside the realm of mathematics there is never any formal connexion between what we describe as 'our evidence' and our conclusions. The problem still remains to be considered how, if not formally, evidence and conclusions are related. And Hume's answer, of course, is that their connexion consists in the fact that we cannot help—the necessity being psychological, not logical—under certain circumstances having certain expectations. If we are asked to justify causal inferences, all we can do is to describe how men actually think.

At the same time, Hume is not altogether happy in this conclusion. There is, on this point, an inner tension in the *Treatise*. In his sceptical moods, Hume insists on the irrationality of causal inference; we can discuss the psychological origins of our inferences, but can go no further: 'all our reasonings concerning causes and effects are deriv'd from nothing but custom; and belief is more properly an act of the sensitive, than of the cogitative part of our natures' (T, 183,. But this tendency in his thinking, however congenial it may be as a stick with which to beat the physicist, threatens the whole conception of a science based upon experience; it emphasizes man, at the cost of making a science of man impossible; it destroys the positive methodology of the *Treatise*. Methodology is not logic; is it therefore caprice?

NOTE. Some critics have found it hard to believe that Hume really meant that syllogistic reasoning, as distinct from demonstration, was restricted to mathematics. I have tried to give the background to this view in 'Descartes, the British Empiricists and Formal Logic' (*Phil. Rev.*, Vol. LXII, No. 4, October 1953, pp. 545–53). The crucial point is that logic has to appear as part of 'the science of human nature'. Of course, the issues were not clear when Hume wrote; to speak of him as 'reducing psychology to logic', is so far misleading that neither psychology nor an entirely non-psychologistic logic had yet been worked out. But it is natural to express Hume's major point in these terms: for it is that there is no such thing (outside mathematics) as formal validity; that logic is a theory of the circumstances in which we draw certain conclusions; that what it is about is the ways in which our minds move from one idea to another. On the two senses of 'resemblance', I am now inclined to think that Hume's problems may be connected with the difficulty of distinguishing between 'categories' and 'classes'. (See the last chapter of my *Philosophical Reasoning*, 1961.)

CHAPTER III

THE METHODOLOGIST

Descartes set out to 'build anew from the foundation' in order to establish 'a firm and permanent structure in the sciences'; Bacon intended 'to try the whole thing anew upon a better plan, and to commence a total reconstruction of sciences, arts, and all human knowledge, raised upon the proper foundations'.[1] In Hume, these seventeenth-century formulae persist; he tells us that he proposes to erect 'a compleat system of the sciences, built on a foundation almost entirely new, and the only one upon which they can stand with any security' (T, xx). And he takes over the assumption, common to Bacon and to Descartes, that 'a new foundation' will consist in a new scientific method. Hume's scheme for reconstruction, however, is very different from that of his predecessors.

The 'security' which Bacon and Descartes sought was an absolute one; the Cartesian method consists of 'certain and simple rules, such that, if a man observe them accurately, he shall never assume what is false as true'.[2] With their help, Descartes thought, science could be so constructed that it would consist 'in its entirety' of 'true and evident cognition'.[3] Such aspirations Hume rejected as chimerical; only pure mathematics, on his view, can achieve absolute certainty; no method can wholly protect the empirical scientist against error. If the scientist were content to contemplate his own perceptions, then, indeed, he could rest secure, but then, too, he would have no need of method. The scientist needs method in order to pass beyond immediately-given perceptions; and as soon as he takes that step security has slipped from his grasp.

When Hume proclaims that his method is 'the only one upon which they [the sciences] can stand with any security', he is deliberately arousing expectations, in order the more effectively to show that they cannot be fulfilled. The most his

[1] *Meditations* I (I, 144); *The Great Instauration*, Proemium.
[2] *Regulae*, IV (I, 9). [3] *Regulae*, IV (I, 3).

method can offer us is security against 'fictions'—or, more accurately, against the *vicious* fictions of metaphysics and superstition, as distinct from those harmless, and even laudable, fictions which are essential to the conduct of life. And the method which thus protects us is not axiomatic in structure but experimental; it rests upon experience, not upon self-evident propositions.

Such a method had already been sketched by Sir Isaac Newton, in his *Rules of Reasoning in Philosophy*.[1] Hume was prepared to acquiesce in the prevailing opinion that 'my lord Bacon' was 'the father of experimental physics' (A, 7); the fact remains that Newton, rather than Bacon, was Hume's master.[2] In his *History of England* (Chapter 71) he describes Newton as 'the greatest and rarest genius that ever arose for the ornament and instruction of the species'; as we have already seen, it was Hume's ambition to be the Newton of the moral sciences. And this in two respects: first, by working out a bold general theory of the mind—his associationism—comparable to Newton's theory of attraction, and secondly, what is our more immediate concern, by extending the Newtonian method to the moral sciences. Many puzzling features of Hume's methodology become less puzzling when we set them in the context of the Newtonian rules.

One of these rules, the third, is distinguished by Hume as 'Newton's chief rule of philosophizing'. It runs as follows: 'the qualities of bodies, which admit neither intension nor remission of degrees, and which are found to belong to all bodies within the reach of our experiments, are to be esteemed the universal qualities of all bodies whatsoever.' Newton goes on to expand the rule thus: 'since the qualities of bodies are only known to us by experiments, we are to hold for universal all such as universally agree with experiments; and such as are not liable to diminution can never be quite taken away. We are certainly not to relinquish the evidence of experiments for the sake of dreams and vain fictions of our own devising; nor are we to

---

[1] *Mathematical Principles*, Bk III (Vol. II, pp. 160-2).

[2] He refers to Bacon twice in the *Enquiries* (129, 219) but not at all in the *Treatise*.

recede from the analogy of Nature, which uses to be simple, and always consonant to itself.'

One is at first somewhat surprised to find that Hume should place such emphasis upon this Newtonian rule; Hume is so much, in text-books, the arch-enemy of generalization that one does not expect him to stress the principle of parsimony. Yet his allegiance to it is unquestionable. 'It is', he says, 'entirely agreeable to the rules of philosophy, and even of common reason; where any principle has been found to have a great force and energy in one instance, to ascribe to it a like energy in all similar instances' (E, 204). The 'simplicity' of his account of the origins of pride is, he considers, a powerful argument in its favour (T, 282); by reference to this same rule he supports the view that considerations of utility play a part in all our moral judgments (E, 204); he regularly appeals on behalf of his associationism, as Newton did on behalf of attraction, to the virtues of generalization.[1]

The contrast between Hume and Berkeley, on this point, is instructive. Berkeley writes: 'Gravitation or mutual attraction because it appears in many instances, some are straightway for pronouncing universal.' It is a major weakness of Newtonian science, on Berkeley's view, that it too much encourages 'that eagerness of the mind, whereby it is carried to extend its knowledge to general theorems'. We should be content to recognize that God acts sometimes in one way, sometimes in another, 'just as He sees convenient'.[2] Berkeley is genuinely suspicious of scientific generalizations; Hume is as intent upon encouraging generalization as Berkeley is upon limiting its employment. Yet at the same time Hume insists upon our inability to demonstrate either that Nature is in fact 'consonant to itself', or that, in any particular case, we are justified, in the demonstrative sense of that word, in generalizing. The methodological problem, then, is to discover a non-demonstrative justification of scientific generalizations.

---

[1] Newton insists, however, on the need for demonstrating that the conformity does in fact hold, by the use of experimental evidence (*Opticks*, p. 76). For Hume's use of the principle see, for example, T, 290.

[2] *Principles*, § 106.

In his comments on his third rule, Newton had already suggested an answer to this problem: scientific generalizations are justified in a sense in which the speculations of the metaphysicians are not, just because, as Newton put it, scientific generalizations 'universally agree with experience'. The significance of this doctrine is more clearly brought out in his fourth rule: 'In experimental philosophy we are to look upon propositions collected by general induction from phaenomena as accurately or very nearly true, notwithstanding any contrary hypothesis that may be imagined, till such time as other phaenomena occur, by which they may either be made more accurate, or liable to exceptions. This rule we must follow that the argument of induction may not be evaded by hypotheses.' 'Agreement with experience', then, consists in 'induction from phaenomena'; induction is the method of justifying scientific generalizations. In the *Opticks*, Newton describes this inductive method as the method of analysis. 'This analysis', he says, 'consists in making experiments and observations, and in drawing general conclusions from them by induction, and admitting of no objections against the conclusions, but such as are taken from experiments or other certain truths. For hypotheses are not to be regarded in experimental philosophy.'[1]

Hume obviously has this passage in mind when, in the *Abstract*, he describes the methods of the 'author of the *Treatise*', who, he says, 'promises to draw no conclusions but where he is authorized by experience' and who 'talks with contempt of hypotheses' (A, 6). Yet, on the face of it, this is a quite inaccurate description of Hume's actual procedure in the *Treatise*. For he there makes free use of hypotheses (under that name)—even, and indeed especially, in that most Newtonian section of the *Treatise*: Book II, *Of the Passions*. He deliberately employs such phrases as the following: 'to illustrate this hypothesis . . .' (T, 289); 'which analogy must be allowed to be no despicable proof of both hypotheses . . .' (T, 290); 'these phaenomena will be found convincing proofs of this hypothesis . . .' (T, 345). Peculiar expressions, these, in the mouth of a man who 'talks with contempt of hypotheses'!

[1] *Query 34*, p. 404.

45

If, indeed, we take literally what Newton says about 'hypotheses', then Hume could not have condemned hypotheses without rejecting the whole of empirical science. Newton wrote: 'whatever is not deduced from the phaenomena is to be called an hypothesis.'[1] And it is, of course, the crucial point in Hume's logic that no empirical generalization can be 'deduced from the phaenomena'. In so far as Newton's theory of 'analytic induction' was an attempt to show that empirical scientific propositions (in distinction from 'hypotheses') were actually implied by the phaenomena—a doctrine which lies behind Newton's regular description of such propositions as 'conclusions'—it was precisely the kind of view which Hume set out to overthrow.

But Newton partly shook himself free from the Baconian conception of induction. Bacon did not doubt that induction amounts to demonstration. 'What the sciences stand in need of', he wrote, 'is a form of induction which shall analyse experience and take it to pieces, and by a due process of exclusion and rejection lead to an inevitable conclusion'.[2] For all that Newton so often describes induction as 'deduction from phaenomena', he did not share Bacon's complete confidence in the inductive method. On occasions, he expresses himself very much in Hume's manner: 'although the arguing from experiments and observations by induction be no demonstration of general conclusions; yet it is the best way of arguing which the nature of things admits of.'[3] If 'deduction' means no more than 'inference from', then Hume would agree that the 'best method of arguing' is deduction from experience, although he would insist that experience does not actually *imply* the conclusions which are derived from it. And if a 'hypothesis' means no more than a proposition which is suggested by, and tested in, experience, then neither Hume nor Newton—if we make allowance for the fact that Newton is only half emancipated from Baconianism—would wish to expel hypotheses from science.

Why then does Newton say that 'hypotheses are not to be

[1] *Principles*, II, 314.
[2] *The Great Instauration*, p. 22 (McKeon's edition).
[3] *Opticks*, p. 404.

regarded in natural philosophy', and of what, precisely, does Hume 'talk with contempt'? Newton is anxious to insist that hypotheses cannot properly be used as a way of avoiding experimental evidence. In examining a 'conclusion', we must pay attention to those 'experiments and other certain truths' which might refute it. But the mere fact that it is possible to *imagine* an hypothesis which would contradict our 'conclusion' need not in the least perturb us. 'Not regarding hypotheses' means not admitting it as an objection to a scientific proposition that it conflicts with some abstractly possible state of affairs. To put the matter in personal terms, Newton is not interested in critics of his theory of attraction who merely point out that it conflicts with this or that speculative hypothesis; criticism must take the form of bringing forward facts which conflict with his theory.

It is here presumed that there is no difficulty in recognizing a 'fact' as something quite distinct from an 'hypothesis'. 'Facts' are what are discovered by experiments and observations; these, it is supposed, contain no tincture of speculation. In the same way, when Hume complains that 'the philosophy of the ancients' is 'entirely hypothetical', he means that it depends 'more upon invention than experience'.[1] And he condemns 'hypothetical arguments, or reasonings upon a supposition' on the ground that they lack 'the authority either of the memory or the senses', the assumption being that the memory and senses present us with indisputable facts (T, 83). Hume was, I think, genuinely perturbed when the course of his argument threatened this clear-cut distinction between facts and speculations. 'I begun this subject with premising', he wrote, 'that we ought to have an implicit faith in our senses, and that this wou'd be the conclusion, I shou'd draw from the whole of my reasoning. But to be ingenuous, I feel myself *at present* of a quite contrary sentiment, and am more inclin'd to repose no faith at all in my senses, or rather imagination, than to place in it such an implicit confidence' (T, 217). 'My senses, or rather imagination . . .', for Hume has discovered difficulties in the view that the senses present us with clear-cut bare facts. It is

[1] *Letters*, Vol. I, p. 16.

only in his moods of 'excessive scepticism', however, that Hume takes this new doctrine with any real seriousness. His general conclusion is still that 'none but a fool or madman will ever pretend to dispute the authority of experience' (E, 36), and that sound methodology will denounce hypotheses which refuse to accept experience as the supreme authority.

To return to Newton, there is a second sense in which 'hypotheses are not to be regarded in natural philosophy': no proposition forms part of science unless it either describes an experiment or has been deduced from experiments. The crucial point is that science has no need of explanations, in the sense of *ad hoc* hypotheses which are constructed simply in order to make experiments 'intelligible'. An hypothesis to which no exceptions have been found satisfies every scientific canon. 'If no exception occur from phaenomena, the conclusion may be pronounced generally.'[1] We ought not, for example, to object to attraction on the ground that we cannot 'see how' it could take place; 'intelligibility' is not a scientific criterion.

Newton's view in the *Principles* is that 'hypotheses whether physical or metaphysical, whether of occult qualities or mechanical, have no place in experimental philosophy'.[2] The contrast between 'occult' and 'mechanical' hypotheses (explanations) is, nevertheless, an important one. The characteristic feature of explanation by occult qualities is that it is merely verbal. 'To tell us that every species of things is endow'd with an occult specifical quality, by which it acts and produces natural effects, is to tell us nothing.'[3] This was, of course, a common criticism of occult qualities, which Hume was content to repeat. 'Occult qualities', according to Hume, are a form of consolation with which Nature has endowed philosophers 'amid all their disappointments and afflictions.' 'They need only say', he continues, 'that any phaenomenon which puzzles them arises from a faculty or an occult quality, and there is an end of all dispute and inquiry upon the matter' (T, 224). 'Faculties' and 'occult qualities' are, indeed, the outstanding examples of what, in the *Enquiry*, Hume calls 'mere conjecture and hypothesis' (E, 145), which are characterized

[1] *Opticks*, p. 404.   [2] II, 314.   [3] *Opticks*, p. 401.

48

by the fact that nothing except what we already know can be inferred from them. In other words, they are *ad hoc* explanations, not genuine scientific hypotheses.

'Mechanical' hypotheses are in a rather different position; and on their role in science Hume and Newton do not agree. The fact is that Newton has a good deal of the rationalist in him: a science which is purely descriptive is, in his eyes, so far incomplete. Bacon had written: 'the most general principles of Nature ought to be held merely positive, as they are discovered, and cannot with truth be referred to a cause',[1] but Newton, as we have already seen, regularly talks about the 'causes' of gravitation. 'For we must learn from the phaenomena of Nature what bodies attract one another, and what are the laws and properties of the attraction, before we enquire the cause by which the attraction is performed.'[2] Although he insists that description must come first, and that it must not be dismissed simply on the ground that it fails to explain, he still contemplates 'explanation' as the final goal. In the *Opticks*, he is prepared to make considerable concessions, even in the main body of the text (the appended *Queries* are confessedly speculative), to 'those who are averse from assenting to any new discoveries, but such as they can explain by an hypothesis'.[3] The *Principles* is more rigorous—perhaps because his critics had shown themselves to be incapable of distinguishing his passing suggestions from his worked-out doctrine. But even in the *Principles*, after firmly announcing that 'I frame no hypotheses', he goes on to say that 'we might add something concerning a certain most subtle spirit which pervades and lies hid in all gross bodies.' He restrains himself from expanding this theory in detail, but only on the ground that he is not 'furnished with that sufficiency of experiments which is required to an accurate determination and demonstration of the laws by which this electric and elastic spirit operates'.[4] There is no intrinsic objection to hypotheses of this sort, as there is to 'occult qualities', although they have no place in *science* until they can be supported by experimental evidence.

Newton never questions that there is an ultimately intelligible

[1] *Aphorisms*, Book I, No. 48.   [2] *Opticks*, p. 376.   [3] p. 280.   [4] II, 314.

scheme of things, in the sense that if we only knew enough we should see why everything must be as it is. That is why he never doubts that there is a 'cause' of gravity. Bodies attract one another as the inverse square of their distance; this is a brute fact; to know its cause would be to see that this is how they must act. The same assumption operates in the work of Boyle, 'whose business', he says, 'is not to explain the adequate cause of the spring of the air, but only to manifest that air hath a spring and to relate some of its effects'.[1] An 'adequate cause' would show us that air must have a spring; Boyle clearly thinks there are such causes, even if physical science does not discover them.

Very often, Hume writes precisely in the manner of Boyle and Newton. The 'causes' of association, he says, are 'mostly unknown' and 'nothing is more requisite for a true philosopher, than to restrain the intemperate desire of searching into causes, and having establish'd any doctrine upon a sufficient number of experiments, rest contented with that, when he sees a farther examination would lead him into obscure and uncertain speculations' (T, 13). Similarly, 'the ultimate cause of impressions' is 'perfectly inexplicable by human reason' (T, 84). More generally, 'no philosopher who is rational and modest has ever pretended to assign the ultimate cause of any natural operation' (E, 30). 'An ultimate cause' is here equivalent to Boyle's 'adequate cause'; to assign an ultimate cause would be to discover a 'connexion' as distinct from a 'conjunction' i.e. to show that the 'natural operation' *must* be what it is. It is assumed, throughout such passages as these, that there are 'ultimate causes' which, unfortunately, we are incapable of apprehending, and Hume finds this assumption a useful prop to his scepticism.

The fact remains that the main tenor of his methodology leads him away, on this point, from Boyle and Newton. Empirical science, to Hume, is the discovery that things in fact behave in certain ways; and it is not our incapacity which prevents us from discovering ultimate causes, but the fact that

[1] *Spring and Weight of the Air*, Experiment I (Collected Works, 1772, Vol. 1).

there are no such causes to discover. No connexion is any more rational than any other; all causes are equally 'adequate', or, from the point of view of a rationalist, equally inadequate. 'Seeing why' a thing behaves as it does would mean seeing that its actions and effects flow from its inner nature. Newton and Locke had recognized that, in Newton's words, 'inward substances are not to be known either by our senses or by any reflex act of our minds';[1] but they still took as their ideal an empirical knowledge which penetrates to the inner nature of things. Hume, at least in his more revolutionary moods, rejects this ideal. There are no 'inward natures' to be apprehended. Description is not second-best science; it is science at its best. In this respect Hume's 'contempt for hypotheses' cuts deeper than Newton's. 'Any hypothesis', he writes, 'that pretends to discover the ultimate original qualities of human nature, ought at first to be rejected as presumptuous and chimerical' (T, xxi). Newton put such hypotheses aside regretfully, as not yet 'deducible from the phaenomena'; Hume rejects them outright. For it is impossible to go beyond experience, and experience does not reveal to us 'ultimate' (i.e. self-explanatory) connexions, but only conjunctions which, however general, are still brute facts. This position he does not always adhere to—
—often enough he speaks as a Lockian, contrasting our actual with a conceivable experience—but the rejection of the rationalistic ideal of explanation is certainly the most important tendency in his methodology.

The question still remains: in what sense, precisely, is our experience 'evidence for' the truth of scientific generalizations? Newton identified 'induction from experience' with 'deduction from phaenomena'. Hume denied that arguments from experience could ever be deductive. Was it possible to give an account of such arguments which would distinguish them from 'dreams and visions'? Unless this is in some sense possible, a science based upon experience is no better than one based upon mere invention; and the moral scientist is as much a visionary as the most superstitious 'enthusiast'.

All 'arguments from experience', on Hume's view, take the

[1] *Principles*, II, 312-13.

form of causal inferences. And it is because Newton adhered to the same doctrine that his first two 'rules for philosophizing' set down conditions under which one thing could be regarded as the cause of another. The first rule asserted that a cause must be necessary for the effect it is said to produce ('Nature is pleased with simplicity and affects not the pomp of superfluous causes'), the second that 'to the same natural effects we must as far as possible assign the same causes'. These two rules are not sharply distinguished from the third rule: 'Nature uses to be simple, and is always consonant with herself' i.e. Nature works with necessary and sufficient conditions.

Hume's 'rules by which to judge of causes and effects' (T, 173) are a considerable development of Newton's. The first three rules assert that the cause must be (1) contiguous to, (2) prior to, (3) constantly conjoined with, the effect; the fourth rule asserts that a cause must be both sufficient and necessary to produce its supposed effect; the fifth, that if different objects seem to produce the same effect, the real cause must be some property they have in common ; the sixth, that if an effect arises from X and not from Y, there must be a point of difference between X and Y, which will be the cause of the effect; the seventh, that if an effect increases or diminishes when corresponding changes take place in the cause, the absence or presence of one part of the cause must be attended by the absence or presence of a *proportionate* part of the effect; the eighth, that if an object exists for any period of time without a certain object following, it cannot be the cause of the object. This is a heterogeneous collection, in part defining 'cause', in part anticipating Mill's 'Uniformity of Nature', in part stating his 'canons of induction'.

All the 'rules' are freely employed by Hume, sometimes in an extremely elaborate fashion, as in the 'Experiments to confirm this system' which make up Book II, Part II, Chapter II of the *Treatise*. In his actual use of them, they come even closer to Mill's canons. Thus, discussing love and hatred, he remarks that 'when the absence of an object or quality removes any usual or natural effect, we may certainly conclude that its presence contributes to the production of the effect' (T, 380), which is substantially Mill's 'method of difference'. Or again, in his essay *Of Interest*, he writes thus; 'An effect always holds proportion with its cause. Prices have risen near four times since the discovery of the Indies; and 'tis probable gold and silver have multiply'd much more: But interest has not fallen much above half. The rate of interest, therefore, is not derived from the quantity of the precious metals'.[1] This is Mill's method of 'concomitant variations', which is already suggested by rule seven.

It is one thing to expound and employ such rules as these: it is another thing to justify their use, or to give an account of their logical status. There are complications at this point which are as embarrassing for Hume as they had been for Newton and were to be for Mill.[2] This is perhaps the explanation of an interesting point of difference between the *Treatise* and the *Enquiry*. Whereas in the *Treatise* Hume's critique is directed as much against the possibility of demonstrating that every event has a cause as against the possibility of demonstrating that A (in particular) is the cause of B, in the *Enquiry* the general causal principle is not critically considered. Selby-Bigge found in this omission evidence of 'the lower philosophical standard of the later work'.[3] The explanation, I suggest, lies rather in Hume's determination, in the later work, to insist upon the broad tendency of his argument. For a variety of reasons, he must press the point that an effect is never deducible from its cause; but he is anxious to say nothing which might suggest that a cause is perhaps not always necessary, that absolute contingency is conceivable. The view that the effect is never deducible from the cause is, in Hume's opinion, a bulwark of science. With its help, he could reply to Berkeley's[4] criticism of science—that it discovers only uniformities and never 'real causes'—and he could cut beneath what was, he thought, a major assumption of the libertarian argument against determinism—that if human actions have a cause, we ought to be able to deduce

[1] G.G., III, 321.

[2] On Newton, cf. E. A. Burtt, *The Metaphysical Foundations of Modern Science*, p. 215.   [3] Introduction to his edition of the *Enquiry*, p. xiv.

[4] *Principles*, § 101 ff.

from the *nature* of human beings how they will behave. 'Being once convinced that we know nothing farther of causation of any kind than merely the *constant conjunction* of objects and the consequent inference of the mind from one to another . . . we may be more easily led to own the same necessity common to all causes' (E, 92). On the other hand, to question whether every event has a cause is to undermine science of every kind, moral no less than physical, and to leave the way open for enthusiasm and superstition.

Hume would not happily accept the suggestion, now current, that methodological rules are simply 'recommendations' or 'proposals'. For, on that showing, the 'superstitious' might simply refuse to accept his recommendations. They might prefer their own proposals, and thus escape his criticism. Hume wants to show that there is some sort of impropriety or irrationality in superstition, whereas *his* rules are intrinsically rational, and in accordance with the nature of reality. He is not content to point out that belief in free will, for example, involves the rejection of his rules; this belief, he considers, is objectively false. In his polemical crusade against superstition (and in the actual conduct of his investigations into the moral sciences) he never doubts that his rules have some sort of objective justification—although, as we shall see later, there are occasions in the *Treatise* at which his own argument compels him to regard all such rules as 'prejudices'.

Can we say that methodological rules are derived from experience? This is explicitly asserted in the *Treatise*: 'these rules are form'd on the nature of our understanding, and on our experience of its operations in the judgments we form concerning objects' (T, 149). Yet 'experience' cannot here be interpreted in what is, for Hume, its usual sense. For we could only learn by experience that a cause is always necessary if there were a constant conjunction between objects and their causes. But Hume admits that causes may be 'secret and concealed'(T, 130). Experience does not always reveal constant conjunctions and hence, on Hume's general theory, the *invariable* habit of expecting a cause could never arise out of experience.

'Experience', then, must now have a special meaning, and such a meaning is vaguely conveyed by Hume's phrase that these rules 'are formed on the nature of our understanding'. The understanding itself is defined as 'the general and more establish'd properties of the imagination' (T, 267). Hume's account of 'general rules' would then run thus: there is such a thing as orderly, or systematic, or philosophical thinking; when we examine the nature of that thinking we discover regularities in it which can be formulated as rules. To say that there are rules 'by which we ought to regulate our judgment concerning causes and effects' (T, 149) is to affirm no more than that, unless we proceed in certain ways, our thinking—and hence, our 'world'—will be unsystematic and disorderly. Thus Hume distinguishes those principles of the imagination which are 'the foundation of all our thoughts and actions, so that upon their removal human nature must immediately perish and go to ruin'—and which are therefore 'received by philosophy'—from those others 'which are observ'd only to take place in weak minds' (T, 225). On this showing, the 'rationality' of general rules consists in their making possible consistent and orderly thinking. To reject the rules, therefore, is not merely to refuse to accept Hume's 'recommendations'; it involves the rejection of any sort of orderly thinking. There is no alternative set of rules which could with equal force be formulated. If we tried to turn superstitious thinking into a set of rules we should find that such rules, 'being opposite to the other principles of custom and reasoning', would soon be 'subverted by a due contrast and opposition' (T, 225).

We are now confronted by a new species of rational inference, which can be distinguished both from the deductive rationality of mathematics and from the irrationality of metaphysics and superstition. Its leading characteristic is regularity; the greater the regularity upon which it rests, the greater its rationality. And so, when this methodological intention—the definition of empirical rationality—is paramount, Hume abandons a dual, in favour of a triple, logic. It is a mistake, he suggests, to describe all our arguments from cause and effect as 'probabilities', although 'in the precedent part of this discourse, I have follow'd this method of expression' (T, 124). 'Common discourse' recognizes that 'many arguments from causation exceed probability, and may be receiv'd as a superior kind of evidence.' 'One wou'd appear ridiculous', he continues, 'who wou'd say, that 'tis only probable the sun will rise to-morrow, or that all men must dye.' It will be 'more convenient' to distinguish two kinds of probability, thus dividing 'human reason into three kinds' viz. knowledge, proofs ('those arguments, which are deriv'd from the relation of cause and effect, and which are entirely free from doubt and uncertainty') and probabilities ('that evidence, which is still attended with uncertainty').

In Boswell's account of his final interview with Hume there is a passage which brings out very clearly the distinction on which Hume is here insisting. 'I asked him', writes Boswell, 'if it was not possible there might be a future state. He answered that it was possible that a piece of coal put upon the fire would not burn; and he added that it was a most unreasonable fancy that he should exist for ever.'[1] It is *possible* that coal put upon the fire will not burn, in the sense that no one can *demonstrate* that it must burn. But the reasonable belief is that it will *in fact* burn, for this is the belief which our experience supports. Immortality, on the other hand, is an 'unreasonable fancy'. Constant conjunctions tell against it, and none tell for it. Nothing which is conceivable is impossible, and the opposite of an empirical proposition is always conceivable; it does not follow, Hume is here suggesting, that one empirical proposition is as good as another. 'There are many different kinds of certainty; and some of them as satisfactory to the mind, tho' perhaps not so regular, as the demonstrative kind';[2] or, again, 'the proof against a miracle, as it is founded on invariable experience, is of that species or kind of proof, which is full and certain when taken alone, because it implies no doubt, as is the case with all probabilities'.[3] To say that 'it is only probable that the sun will rise to-morrow' will 'appear ridiculous' unless we have some positive reason for believing that it might not rise. Here

---

[1] Reprinted in *Dialogues*, p. 77 (ed. Kemp Smith).
[2] *Letters*, I, 187.   [3] *Ibid.*, I, 350.

56

Hume is at his closest to Butler, who, describing 'argument from analogy', wrote that 'this way of arguing is evidently natural, just and conclusive. For there is no man can make a question but that the sun will rise to-morrow.'[1]

When, therefore, critics like A. E. Taylor maintain that 'the naturalist who derides his neighbour's groundless anticipations of the joys of Paradise forgets that his own anticipation that the sun will rise to-morrow is equally groundless',[2] they are ignoring an important tendency in Hume's thinking. To 'give a ground', Hume might reply, is to point to a conjunction from which our belief is derived. There is such a conjunction (and an invariable one) in the case of the sun's rising; there is no such conjunction (not even a variable one) in the case of our expectation of the joys of Paradise—this, then, is a 'groundless fancy'. Certainly, there is no 'ground' in either case, in the sense in which the rationalist demands a ground, but the rationalist must learn, Hume would say, to abate his unreasonable demands.

At the same time Taylor could quote, in support of his interpretation, a passage from the *Enquiry*: 'While we cannot give a satisfactory reason, why we believe, after a thousand experiments, that a stone will fall, or fire burn; can we ever satisfy ourselves concerning any determination, which we may form, with regard to the origin of worlds, and the situation of nature from, and to, eternity?' (E, 162). This is one of those occasions on which Hume is mainly concerned to subdue the ambitions of cosmogonists; at such times it suits him to use the phrase 'a satisfactory reason' in such a way that only those reasons are satisfactory which can serve as premises in demonstrative arguments to the required conclusion.[3] But this is not merely an *argumentum ad hominem*; he is never quite sure whether constant conjunction can properly be described as a 'satisfactory reason' for believing in universal connexions.

Hume's own hesitations on this point are clearly illustrated

[1] *Analogy*, Introduction.
[2] 'Hume on the Miraculous' (*Philosophical Studies*, p. 355).
[3] cf. G. E. Moore's 'Hume's Philosophy' and his 'The Nature and Reality of Objects of Perception', both in his *Philosophical Studies*.

in his theory of probability. He begins by describing what he calls 'philosophical probability'. There is a slide, he at first suggests, from probability to proof. 'As the habit, which produces the association, arises from the frequent conjunction of objects, it must arrive at its perfection by degrees, and must acquire new force from each instance, that falls under our observation. The first instance has little or no force: the second makes some addition to it: the third becomes still more sensible; and 'tis by these slow steps, that our judgment arrives at a full assurance' (T, 130). So far, then, the suggestion is that the mere aggregation of instances constitutes the difference between probability and proof; at some undefined point the number of instances is so large that they together constitute an empirical proof. He is not content to say, merely, that at a certain point our hesitations disappear. A small number of instances, he says, 'is *only to be esteem'd* a presumption or probability'; the difference lies between '*kinds of evidence*';[1] he writes as if the number of instances were, in an objective sense, 'evidence'.

There is one obvious difficulty in this view, viz. that propositions are sometimes established by a single instance, or a small number of instances. Hume is very conscious of this fact; he is led to conclude that 'no one who is arriv'd at the age of maturity' is ever acquainted with a probability based simply on the number of positive instances. 'What we have found once to follow from any object, we conclude will forever follow from it.' We are content with 'one single experiment, when duly prepar'd and examin'd' (T, 131). Hume finds himself in a dilemma. It would suit him best, with his theory that causal expectations are habits, to regard the number of cases as the determining factor; yet he feels obliged to admit that a single case can provoke an expectation, and can be as good a ground as a number of cases. Now, if causal inferences are to be mechanical reactions, Hume cannot say that sometimes one case is enough, whereas at other times more are needed—this would raise the awkward question what the difference can be between the two cases. He concludes, therefore—in obvious

[1] T, 131. My italics in both quotations.

conflict with the facts—that one case alone is necessary, once the general habit of expecting to find constant conjunctions has been firmly established in our minds.

'Probable reasoning', then, in a mature person arises out of the experience of positive irregularities, not merely out of the fact that only a small number of instances has been examined. In all cases of irregularity the 'philosopher' seeks a 'secret cause' which accounts for the irregularities, whereas the 'vulgar' are content to assume that, in this particular instance, the regular cause has simply failed to operate. But although there is this difference in the method by which men explain irregularities, the structure of the probable reasoning we employ is in all the cases the same. If the constancy of the union is irregular, we hesitate to predict the future with any certainty; and similarly, in the case of analogy, an imperfect resemblance between the instances which confront us will affect the confidence of our prediction. 'If you weaken either the union or resemblance, you weaken the principle of transition, and of consequence that belief, which arises from it' (T, 142). This is the general principle which underlies all probable reasoning.

By now Hume has converted logic into psychology. If we ask why we have not sufficient 'evidence' when the union is 'weakened', Hume's answer is simply that this is how our minds happen to work. Anything which weakens the associative links between our ideas will help to destroy our confidence in the beliefs which such links generate. And he goes on to develop this answer in a sceptical direction. The 'kinds of probability' he has so far been discussing are 'receiv'd by philosophers, and allow'd to be reasonable foundations of belief and opinion' (T, 143). It is generally agreed that it is 'reasonable' to argue from analogy, and from a large proportion of positive cases. Other kinds of probability are regarded as unphilosophical. 'They have not', as Hume expresses the matter, 'had the good fortune to obtain the same sanction.' To take one case, 'the argument, which we found on any matter of fact we remember, is more or less convincing, according as the fact is recent or remote'. This difference is not accepted by philosophers as 'solid and legitimate'. But whatever philosophers may say, 'this circumstance has a considerable influence on the understanding, and secretly changes the authority of the same argument, according to the different times, in which it is propos'd to us' (T, 143).

'Unphilosophical probability' depends upon a trick of the mind; but so does philosophical probability. Why, then, does the philosopher regard them so differently? The answer cannot be that 'X is usually Y' is good evidence for 'this X will probably be Y', whereas 'the conjunction of X with Y occurred a long time ago' is not good evidence against 'X is always Y'—at least if by 'good evidence' we mean that the first proposition implies and the second does not imply the conclusion we draw from it. For in neither case, on Hume's view, is there objective implication; in both cases we are led to a certain conclusion as a result of a merely psychological operation: the inconstancy, or the remoteness in time, of a conjunction diminishes the vivacity of the ideas to which it gives rise.

Is there, then, no difference between the two cases? One difference, Hume again suggests, is that to rely upon unphilosophical probability would be to commit ourselves to an 'irregular' kind of reasoning, which is 'capricious and uncertain' in contrast with the 'extensive and constant' principles of philosophical reasoning (T, 149). But why should we prefer regularity to irregularity? To this the only answer can be, Hume replies, that 'the disposition and character of the person' (T, 150) will determine his preference. The 'vulgar' prefer caprice, 'the wise' prefer regularity. Clearly, this is question-begging; it assumes that we already know who 'the wise' are, although it is precisely the point at issue whether there is such a thing as superior wisdom. In the end, then, psychology triumphs. Empirical reasoning fades away; it is found to be nothing more than the habitual procedure of those persons we choose to dignify as 'the wise' or 'the philosophical'. The logical problem—how can empirical reasoning be justified?—vanishes as unanswerable. The only questions which remain fall within the province of the science of man. Under what circumstances are we confident? What are the psychological peculiarities of the man who thinks scientifically—i.e. in the manner we choose to call scientific although such thinking has no formal peculiarities—as distinct from him we call super-stitious? And yet Hume is also uncomfortably aware that to set about answering even these questions is to presume that it is possible, in some sense, to establish a scientific conclusion. The fluctuations in his theory of belief illustrate very clearly the character and the extent of that discomfort. In this case the trend is the other way—from the doctrine that all beliefs are on the same footing to the doctrine that some beliefs are much more rational than others. But the trend is not a consis-tent one; three distinct theories of belief are put forward at a relatively early stage of the *Treatise*; and no one of them is ever finally abandoned.

Theory 1: 'Belief is nothing but a more vivid and intense conception of any idea' (T, 120).

Theory 2: 'Belief may be most accurately defined: A lively idea related to or associated with a present impression' (T, 96).

Theory 3: 'Belief arises only from causation' (T, 107).

'Beliefs' can never be demonstrated; to that doctrine Hume remains faithful. When he wants to emphasize that this is true of all beliefs, those of the physical scientist no less than those of the moralist or aesthetician, Hume places the stress on Theory 1. This theory reaches its fullest expressions in passages like the following: 'All probable reasoning is nothing but a species of sensation. 'Tis not solely in poetry and music, we must follow our taste and sentiment, but likewise in philosophy' (T, 103). Every belief is a vivid perception, and to 'justify' a belief will consist simply in indicating that our perception is genuinely a belief (is conceived in the appropriate way). 'After the most accurate and exact of my reasonings, I can give no reason why I shou'd assent to it; and feel nothing but a *strong* propensity to consider objects *strongly* in that view, under which they appear to me' (T, 265).

This account of belief, however, leaves the door wide open for superstition and enthusiasm. And so it is suggested, in the first place, that a genuine belief must always be somehow related to an impression (Theory 2). This is, in part, a psychological expedient, an attempt to give an account of the means by which certain perceptions come to be endowed with a peculiar vivacity—the vivacity is supposed to be transferred to them from the innately vivid related impression—but it also serves to tie our beliefs down, rooting them in experience. Already, however, 'belief' is coming to have an honorific meaning, to suggest *reasonableness*. For Hume feels obliged to admit that many of our beliefs—in the original, extended meaning of the word—do not derive their vivacity from impressions. This is particularly the case with that important class of beliefs which have their source in 'education', by which Hume means indoctrination. In this case, the simple repetition of an idea is enough to endow it with vividness. 'But', he says, 'as education is an artificial and not a natural cause, and as its maxims are frequently contrary to reason, and even to themselves in different times and places, it is never upon that account recogniz'd by philosophers' (T, 117). 'Recognized' here means 'approved'; and the disapproval of philosophers has its usual origin: education works in an *irregular* way. Hume is not perturbed by the fact that there is a class of 'beliefs' which, although they are vivid, are not associated with an impression; his concern now is only with those 'beliefs' which philosophers are prepared to approve.

Even more honorific is the third theory. If 'belief arises only from causation', if 'we can never be induc'd to believe any matter of fact, except where its cause, or its effect, is present to us' (T, 623), then only a scientifically inferred 'idea' can be a belief, and all other ideas are cast into a nameless darkness. Hume admits that resemblance and contiguity, as well as causation, can enliven ideas; their influence, however, is 'feeble and uncertain', and partakes so much of the nature of 'caprice' that we form a general rule against placing any reliance upon the 'momentary glimpses of light' which they afford us (T, 109-10). A belief is identified with an idea which belongs to 'the system of the judgment', or, in other words, which we take to have a place in what the mind 'dignifies with the title of *realities* (T, 108).

Thus, what set out to be a theory of belief, in something

like the ordinary sense of the word, has become, with no explicit acknowledgment of that fact, a theory of what it is 'rational' to believe. Every belief, it is at first argued, is equally a matter of taste; but Hume ends by sharply distinguishing between 'serious conviction' and 'poetical enthusiasm' (T, 631), with the help of 'general rules' (for all the dubiousness of their own origin). Fancy 'enters into all our reasonings' (T, 140); 'as our assent to all probable reasonings is founded on the vivacity of ideas, it resembles many of those whimsies and prejudices, which are rejected under the opprobious character of being the offspring of the imagination' (T, 117)—so Hume argues. Yet fancy, he wishes also to insist, is very different from scientific thinking.

Let us now reconsider our original question. What, for Hume, is the difference between a good 'general rule'—or methodological principle—and a bad one? The first possible answer is that the good rule is one which is founded upon experience. To this Hume raises two objections. The first is that the rules themselves assert that we ought to rely upon experience and must not, therefore, themselves presume the virtue of that reliance; the second is that 'founded upon experience' cannot mean *implied* by experience because experience implies nothing, and if it means anything less—for example, 'suggested by experience'—we cannot show that the manner in which 'good' rules are suggested to us differs in any vital respect from the manner in which 'bad' rules (those we call 'prejudices') come into being. In either case what happens is simply that some of our ideas are vivified by those conjunctions which we encounter in our experience.

The second possible answer is that 'good' rules enable us to co-ordinate our thinking, to construct a system of the judgment, in a way in which 'bad' rules do not. This Hume very often asserts, but he also draws attention to two major difficulties in this method of discrimination. The first, which we shall discuss in more detail in a later chapter, is that 'bad' rules (which could not be regularized) are as essential to science as good ones. If we determine to 'reject all the trivial suggestions of the fancy', if we 'adhere to the understanding', this decision will be attended with 'the most fatal consequences' (T, 267); we shall be plunged into the deepest scepticism. The second difficulty is that we merely push our original problem further back. We say that a 'good' rule is a regular one. But why should regularity be preferred to irregularity? Can this be anything more than a prejudice on the part of those we choose to consider wise?

Thus, it would seem, 'good' rules cannot be distinguished from mere prejudices. Yet this conclusion, however gratifying it may be to Hume in his more mischievous moods, is one which he would not care regularly to maintain. It is certainly significant that those passages (quoted above) in which he most vigorously insists that there are empirical proofs 'quite as satisfactory' as those of mathematics occur in private letters, away from the sceptical atmosphere of the *Treatise*. These passages express the conviction with which he worked, whether he was denouncing theology or helping to develop the moral sciences. But he left himself with no way of showing that this conviction was anything more than a prejudice; and at some moments, although not at others, he is prepared complacently to acquiesce in this conclusion. The unresolved tension between the sceptic and the scientist here manifests itself in its least disguised form. A general rule is only a propensity; at the same time it is the great scourge of propensities. This 'new and signal contradiction in our reason', arising from the fact that 'the following of general rules is a very unphilosophical species of probability' and yet "tis only by following them that we can correct this, and all other unphilosophical probabilities' is perhaps one which, Hume says, 'the sceptics may have the pleasure of observing' (T, 150). But can a sober moral scientist have the same pleasure in observing it?

CHAPTER IV

THE POSITIVIST

ALMOST alone in this respect among the great philosophers, Hume is occasionally quoted with approval by logical positivists. One passage from the *Enquiry*, in particular, has lent a touch of colour to innumerable positivist writings. 'If we take in our hand any volume; of divinity or school metaphysics, for instance; let us ask, *Does it contain any abstract reasoning concerning quantity or number?* No. *Does it contain any experimental reasoning concerning matter of fact and existence?* No. Commit it then to the flames: for it can contain nothing but sophistry and illusion' (E, 165).

This is a resounding conclusion to the *Enquiry*, but, like most resounding conclusions, it needs to be examined in a sceptical spirit. One must not too lightly assume that it quite accurately conveys the final outcome of Hume's reasoning. Hume is quite prepared to formulate 'general rules' which are neither quantitative nor experimental and to describe them, without compunction, as 'metaphysical'. Thus he feels free to employ 'an establish'd maxim in metaphysics, *that nothing we imagine is absolutely impossible*' (T, 32), or that other maxim, which although it is 'condemned by several metaphysicians' is very important for his theory of perception, '*that an object may exist and yet be nowhere*' (T, 235). No doubt, the status of such maxims is as obscure in Hume's philosophy as it is in Wittgenstein's *Tractatus Logico-Philosophicus*, but Hume did not conclude, in Wittgenstein's manner, that his own book was one of those which ought to be 'cast into the flames'.

The word 'metaphysics' is notoriously obscure; in order to understand the nature, and the limits, of Hume's positivism we must begin by asking against what species of 'metaphysics' it is directed. This question is not an easy one to answer, for his usage was not consistent. Beattie was struck by the ambiguity of 'metaphysics' and was led to distinguish three different senses of the word. In one sense, it includes 'all disquisitions concerning things immaterial', so that 'the plainest account of the faculties of the mind, and of the principles of morals and natural religion would be termed metaphysics'. In a second sense, it means those 'arguments and illustrations in the abstract philosophy, which are not obvious to ordinary understandings'; or thirdly, says Beattie (and he is plainly girding at Hume), metaphysics is 'that mode of abstract investigation, so common among the modern sceptics and the schoolmen, which is supported either by an ambiguous and indefinite phraseology or by that in conjunction with a partial experience'.[1]

Hume's positivism is directed against metaphysics in the third of these senses; he would regard it as a serious criticism of his own work if it could be shown that, as Beattie suggests, it is itself 'a mode of abstract investigation . . . which is supported by ambiguous and indefinite phraseology', for this is precisely what he set out to destroy. 'We must', he says, 'cultivate true metaphysics with some care in order to destroy the false and adulterate', and by 'false' metaphysics he means 'that abstruse philosophy and metaphysical jargon, which, being mixed up with popular superstition, renders it in a manner impenetrable to careless reasoners, and gives it the air of science and wisdom' (E, 12). 'True' metaphysics, in contrast, consists of 'an accurate scrutiny into the powers and faculties of human nature' (E, 13). In Beattie's classification, metaphysics (sense one) must replace metaphysics (sense three). The science of human nature, not abstruse jargon, is *philosophia prima*.

Hume knew, however, that accusations of 'abstruseness' had to be cautiously handled, since much of his own work was abstruse, in the popular sense of the word. In the first of his *Political Discourses*[2] he divides mankind into two classes— shallow thinkers and abstruse thinkers. 'Abstruse thinkers', he says, 'suggest hints, at least and start difficulties'; in contrast, 'an author is little to be valued, who tells us nothing, but what we can learn from every coffee-house conversation'. Shallow thinkers 'are apt to decry even those of *solid* understanding as *abstruse* thinkers and metaphysicians and refiners; and never will

[1] *Essay on Truth*, pp. 403-4.   [2] *Of Commerce*, G.G., III, 287.

allow anything to be just, which is beyond their own weak conceptions'. Hume was well aware that the rejection of 'metaphysics' may be merely a cloak for Philistinism. How, then, can the wrong sort of abstruseness be distinguished from the sort which is admissible and even desirable? A ground of distinction, roughly equivalent to Beattie's distinction between metaphysics (sense two) and metaphysics (sense three), is suggested in *The Principles of Morals*: 'all this is metaphysics, you cry. That is enough; there needs nothing more to give a strong presumption of falsehood. Yes, reply I, here are metaphysics surely; but they are all on your side, who advance an abstruse hypothesis, which can never be made intelligible, nor quadrate with any particular instance or illustration. The hypothesis which we embrace is plain. . . . If you call this metaphysics, and find anything abstruse here, you need only conclude that your turn of mind is not suited to the moral sciences' (E, 289).

The objectionable sort of 'metaphysics', then, is the sort which propounds 'unintelligible' hypotheses, as distinct from hypotheses which are merely difficult to understand. How are we to tell whether an hypothesis is unintelligible? It is at this point, in his theory of meaning, that Hume most closely approaches the positivism of our own day. His critical method is precisely that advocated by Wittgenstein in the *Tractatus Logico-Philosophicus*: 'when someone wished to say something metaphysical, to demonstrate to him that he had given no meaning to certain signs in his propositions' (6.53). As is so often the case, on account of the peculiar purpose and character of that work, the *Abstract* most succinctly describes Hume's procedure. 'When he suspects', wrote Hume concerning 'the author of the *Treatise*', 'that any philosophical term has no idea annexed to it (as is too common) he always asks *from what impression that idea is derived?* And if no impression can be produced, he concludes that the term is altogether insignificant. 'Tis after this method he examines our idea of *substance* and *essence*: and it were to be wished, that this rigorous method were more practised in all philosophical debates' (A, 11).

The general theory of meaning which is here taken for granted is worked out in somewhat greater detail in the

Enquiry. We seek to discover what a word means. We are told that it refers to a certain idea. The idea may be a complex one; if so, we shall enquire into its definition. But a definition is 'nothing but an enumeration of those parts or simple ideas' which compose the complex idea. Suppose we are still dissatisfied, questioning whether there are any simple ideas of the sort to which the definition refers. Then all that remains is to 'produce the impressions or original sentiments from which the ideas are copied'. Our hesitations are now at an end. 'These impressions are all strong and sensible. They admit not of ambiguity' (E, 62). But if this process cannot be carried through, then the word from which we started must have no sense.

It is an important point in Hume's analysis that the problem is always whether a *word* has a meaning. In a secondary sense, we can talk of the meaning of an idea, but with this difference— a word can be meaningless, but there are no meaningless ideas. His insistence on this point stands in sharp contrast to the search, by later positivists, for 'the meaning of a proposition', as if a proposition (in distinction from a set of words) could be meaningless. And the advantage, in this contrast, lies with Hume, as the later history of positivism sufficiently reveals.

One other point of contrast will be obvious. The verifiability principle of the positivists ('the meaning of a proposition lies in the method of its verification') is prospective, predictive; Hume's theory of meaning is retrospective. In Hume's view, an expression is meaningless unless it refers to ideas which have been derived from past experience, whereas for writers like Carnap the test is whether any 'perceptions or feelings or experiences . . . may be expected *for the future*.'[1] There are signs, however, that Hume was working towards the modern formula. Take, for example, his criticism of 'the religious hypothesis' in his essay *Of a Particular Providence and a Future State*. 'No new fact', he says, 'can ever be inferred from the religious hypothesis; no event foreseen or foretold; no reward or punishment expected or dreaded, beyond what is already

---

[1] *Philosophy and Logical Syntax*, p. 15. My italics. William James, similarly, insists on the forward-looking character of his pragmatic theory of meaning as its great point of superiority over any sort of copy-theory.

known by practice and observation' (E, 146). The implication, clearly is that 'the religious hypothesis' is otiose, although he does not care (or perhaps dare) to say that it is 'meaningless'. What is called 'the evidence' for Providence is actually the whole content of the Providential theory. 'I deny a providence, you say . . . but surely I deny not the course itself of events, which lies open to every one's enquiry and examination . . . and what can you say more, allowing all your suppositions and reasonings' (E, 140). This is, indeed, a natural development from that critique of 'hypotheses' which we have already discussed.

In the *Dialogues* this sort of positivist argument is directed against the theory of design. If that theory rests upon experience, as Cleanthes has argued (D, 140), there must be consequences following from it which would not follow from any other hypothesis: we must be able to show that unless the world has been designed by an intelligent designer, it could not possess the characteristics it now displays. 'In this little corner of the world alone', Philo points out, 'there are four principles *reason, generation, instinct, vegetation,* which are similar to each other, and are the causes of similar effects. . . . Any one of these four principles (and a hundred others which lie open to our conjecture) may afford us a theory, by which to judge of the origin of the world' (D, 178). The difficulty does not lie in the invention of a theory, but in showing that one theory is better than another: unless this can be done, every theory is equally an absurdity, 'and it is very indifferent to which we give our preference' (D, 174). There is no 'natural religion'; or, in other words, theology lies completely outside the realm of positive enquiry in which Locke, for example, had tried to give it a place;[1] it rests upon 'invention', not upon 'experience'.

There are, then, obvious resemblances, in spite of divergences

[1] *Essay,* Bk IV, Ch. xxi, 'The end of this [natural philosophy] is bare speculative truth: and whatsoever can afford the mind of man any such falls under this branch, whether it be God himself, angels, spirits, bodies, or any of their affections, as number and figure etc.' Writers like Beattie put natural theology within 'pneumatology ' i.e. the science of mind, on the ground that God is a mind (*Elements of Moral Science,* Introduction, § 7). But Hume is denying that it forms part either of the natural (including the moral) sciences or of the demonstrative sciences—it follows, therefore, that it is not a genuine enquiry at all, but consists merely in guess-work.

at certain points, between Hume's and later positivism. Metaphysical doctrines, both agree, are not to be condemned as false but rather to be rejected as meaningless. They can have meaning only if they point to 'experiences', past or future, only if their being true would 'make a difference' to the kind of experiences we have. And at another point, too, Hume anticipates recent positivism. Metaphysical doctrines, he argues, are interesting only as dreams are interesting. 'Several moralists', he says, 'have recommended it as an excellent method of becoming acquainted with our own hearts . . . to recollect our dreams in a morning, and examine them with the same rigour, that we wou'd our most serious and most deliberate actions' (T, 219). This is the spirit, he goes on to suggest, in which we ought to scrutinize the fictions of the metaphysician; they are useful to us only as illustrations of the way in which the human mind works. (From a very different psychological standpoint, Carnap was to suggest that 'realism is often a symptom of the type of constitution called by the psychologists extraverted.')[1]

In particular, metaphysical doctrines illustrate the tendency of our minds to construct 'fictions', in order to reconcile apparent conflicts in our experience. Hume illustrates this point, in some detail, by considering the case of *substance*. When we watch a thing gradually changing over a period of time, this, Hume argues, is rather like watching what does not change at all; hence we are led to ascribe an 'identity' to the thing in question. We think of a human being, for example, as having a permanent identity. But when we compare the thing after a period of time has elapsed with the thing as it was at the beginning of that period (as when, for example, a time goes by without our encountering an old friend), we notice that considerable changes have taken place. This cuts across our original ascription to the thing of a permanent identity. We have now two contrary inclinations; and we overcome the conflict by feigning 'something unknown and invisible' which, we suppose, persists unchanged beneath the diversity we feel bound to admit; this unknown, invisible something is what we

---

[1] *Philosophy and Logical Syntax*, p. 30.

call 'substance'. By the application of the same methods we gradually construct an entire system of fictions: 'philosophers . . . both suppose a substance supporting, which they do not understand, and an accident supported, of which they have as imperfect an idea' (T, 222). The whole system rests on nothing more solid than 'trivial propensities of the imagination': our tendency to 'overcome' contradictions by constructing imaginary entities. These propensities may carry the metaphysician so far that—as in his talk of 'sympathies and antipathies and horrors of a vacuum'—he ascribes to objects the emotions which he observes in himself, in the manner of children and poets. 'We must pardon children, because of their age; poets, because they profess to follow implicitly the suggestions of their fancy: but what excuse shall we find to justify our philosophers in so signal a weakness?' (T, 225).

Metaphysics, then, arises out of 'trivial', as contrasted with 'regular', tendencies of the imagination—the latter being what we call 'scientific inference'. Under the influence of these tendencies, the imagination generates fictions. These, Hume suggests, as Carnap was to do after him, are like the fancies of the poet, in so far as they are the products of an unfettered imagination. But in another respect they are unlike, a point Carnap was not to make: the fancies of the poets are at least composed of simple ideas and, in the end, of impressions, whereas the fictions of metaphysicians are not ideas at all. They are merely words, 'wholly insignificant and unintelligible' (T, 224). If they seem to have a meaning, this is only because certain features of our experience originally set the imagination at work; in this sense the 'meaning' of Providence is that certain regularities are encountered in our experience; the 'meaning' of substance is that certain regularities approach very closely to identity; the 'meaning' of an occult quality is that a certain problem confronts us. And, Hume would further argue, metaphysics is dangerous, in a sense in which poetry is not. 'Generally speaking, the errors in religion are dangerous; those in philosophy only ridiculous' (T, 272)—but when philosophy provides superstition with a cloak of pseudo-scientific respectability, it, too, comes to be a danger.

71

So much for Hume's critique of metaphysics, which obviously rests on two assumptions: that a meaningful expression always points to an impression, and that 'trivial' can be sharply distinguished from 'regular' imaginative tendencies. If an idea can exist without referring to an impression, then it will never be possible to show that a philosophical 'term' has no idea attached to it; for if anyone likes to assert that he has such an idea, no one can dispute his contention. And if all the tendencies of the imagination are on the same footing, then metaphysics is as firmly founded as science. Thus only after we have explored Hume's phenomenalism and his scepticism will we be able quite to estimate the strength of Hume's critique of metaphysics. He is confident, however, that he has defeated the claim of metaphysics to be the science of sciences. This leaves a vacant throne; he has now to show that the science of man is the rightful occupant of it.

The most inveterate positivist cannot deny that there are philosophical puzzles. These cannot be puzzles about the properties of metaphysical entities. What, then, are they about? And how can they be solved? The answer most contemporary positivists would suggest is that they are about *language*; and that we 'solve' (or, better, *dissolve*) them by pointing to the linguistic confusions out of which they arise.[1]

There are certain passages in Hume which, at first sight, suggest a similar view. The most striking example is his remark that 'the nice and subtile questions concerning personal identity can never possibly be decided, and are to be regarded rather as grammatical than as philosophical difficulties' (T, 262). But the contrast should be noted: grammatical *rather than* philosophical. Although it is a 'grammatical' question whether a house is 'still the same' after extensive renovations have been made to it, the central issues in the controversy about personal identity cannot be so lightly dismissed. 'The controversy concerning identity is not merely a dispute of words' (T, 255). The most notable verbal disputes

---

[1] That such problems should be dissolved, but cannot be solved, is a view ascribed to Wittgenstein by John Wisdom ('Metaphysics and Verification', *Mind*, October, 1938).

are those which are concerned with questions of degree. 'Men may argue to all eternity, whether Hannibal be a great, or a superlatively great man' (D, 217); and, similarly, they may perpetually disagree about whether two things are 'very much alike' or 'precisely the same'. Such disputes need to be distinguished more carefully than they usually are from philosophical disputes proper—'nothing is more usual than for philosophers to encroach upon the province of grammarians' (E, 312)—but only to that extent is the discussion of such verbal points relevant to philosophy.

Of course, it is also important for the philosopher to be clear about the meaning of the expressions he employs, since a failure on this point may give rise to useless disputes. In his essay *Of Liberty and Necessity*, Hume suggests that 'from this circumstance alone, that a controversy has been long kept on foot and remains still undecided, we may presume that there is some ambiguity in the expression, and that the disputants affix different ideas to the terms employed in the controversy' (E, 80). And he sets out to show that 'all men have ever agreed in the doctrine both of necessity, and of liberty, according to any reasonable sense, which can be put on these terms'; 'the whole controversy has hitherto turned merely upon words' (E, 81). The impulse behind this method, however, is Cartesian with no hint of modern linguistic doctrines. To engage fruitfully in controversy we need 'clear ideas'; clear ideas depend upon precise definition (E, 61); and men have not, so far, defined necessity in a precise way. The dispute is verbal only in the sense that controversialists, on both sides of the argument, have wrongly assumed that 'necessity' means 'necessary connexion'; once this assumption is abandoned, Hume argues, liberty and necessity will be found not to be in conflict one with another.

There is nowhere in Hume, then, any suggestion that we can solve philosophical problems by examining or prescribing usages. 'The question being merely verbal', writes Hume of the controversy whether talents can be virtues, 'cannot possibly be of any importance. A moral, philosophical discourse need not enter into all these caprices of language' (E, 314). It is important for philosophers not 'to engage in disputes about words' while imagining that 'they are handling controversies of the deepest importance and concern' (E, 312); but there *are* controversies of the 'deepest importance' which are properly philosophical.

Hume's positivism, then, is not linguistic. At the same time, he would agree with modern positivists that philosophers ask questions which are, as they stand, unanswerable, that they raise problems which, in the ordinary sense of the word, cannot be 'solved'. But we should convert them, on Hume's view, into psychological, not into linguistic, issues. The 'true metaphysics', as we have already pointed out, is 'the accurate scrutiny of human nature'; Hume's positivism substitutes psychology for the traditional metaphysics. 'The logic of science', writes Carnap, 'takes the place of the inextricable tangle of problems known as philosophy.'[1] One must substitute 'science of human nature' for 'logic of science' in order to arrive at Hume's view.

The pattern of Hume's argument, in his own judgment, most triumphantly emerges in his analysis of causation—which is one main reason why the *Abstract* and the *Enquiry* concentrate on this analysis—is somewhat subdued when substance and external existence are his themes, and reaches its nemesis in the analysis of personal identity. But, in fact, the difficulties which Hume detects in his account of personal identity are equally present in his analysis of causality. Let us first consider that analysis. The philosophical problem, as it has usually been formulated, is to describe the necessary connexion between cause and effect. Hume's critical method swings into action. If the expression 'necessary connexion' has a meaning, it must refer to an idea of necessity. From what impression is this idea derived? Suppose we examine causes, in search of their necessary connexion with their effects. Our search is in vain; we find that cause and effect are conjoined, but nothing more; no connexion holds between them. The effect is not discoverable in the cause, so the link between them cannot be a species of logical necessity; nor do we find in the cause anything which

[1] *Logical Syntax of Language*, p. 278.

could be described as its 'power' to produce effects. Hence, Hume concludes, our original problem is unanswerable; we cannot describe the nature of the 'tie' between cause and effect, because there is no such tie to describe.

The fact remains that when A appears, we cannot help expecting its effect, B. How does it happen that, although we do not experience any necessary connexion between A and B, this expectation arises within us? This genuine psychological problem replaces our original philosophical pseudo-problem; and we answer it in psychological terms, making use of the familiar conceptions of association and habit. A and B have been regularly conjoined in the past; this establishes *in us* the habit of expecting B when A confronts us. We have now found the impression of necessity from which our idea of necessary connexion derives; but it lies in us, not in our objects. 'Necessity is the effect of this observation [of constant conjunction] and is nothing but an internal impression of the mind, or a determination to carry our thoughts from one object to another' (T, 165). 'After a repetition of similar instances, the mind is carried by habit, upon the appearance of one event, to expect its usual attendant, and to believe that it will exist. This connexion, therefore, which we *feel* in the mind, this customary transition of the imagination from one object to its usual attendant, is the sentiment or impression from which we form the idea of power or necessary connexion' (E, 75).

We may ask how it happens, under these circumstances, that we ever come to suppose otherwise, why we are ever led to imagine that the necessity attaches to the relation between the cause and the effect, as distinct from the workings of our own mind. Hume's answer is that 'the mind has a great propensity to spread itself on external objects, and to conjoin with them any internal impressions, which they occasion, and which always make their appearance at the same time that these objects discover themselves to the senses' (T, 167). This device, we shall find, is typical; Hume tries to operate with a bold sweeping associationist psychology, but has' constantly to supplement it with subsidiary 'propensities'. There is a suspiciously *ad hoc* air about the supplementation; Hume is well aware of this fact, and is careful to insist that the same propensity can be observed in operation on other occasions. We cannot, therefore, rule it out of court as an 'occult quality', as a mere name for our ignorance, which 'explains' the transfer of necessity by affirming that we have a 'propensity' so to transfer it.

There is a notorious difficulty in this account of causality. Hume sets out to explain what it means to say that 'C is necessarily connected with E'. His explanation runs as follows: 'A person P necessarily thinks of E when he encounters C'. But the real point of difficulty in the explicandum lies in the word 'necessarily', which Hume's analysis simply repeats. If the explanation simply means: 'A person P always thinks of E when he encounters C', then presumably the explicandum means: 'C is always conjoined with E.' Then there is no impression of 'necessary connexion'; this is either a meaningless expression with no idea attached to it or else a synonym for constant conjunction. And this conclusion does not suit Hume in the least, because he will no longer be able to conclude that 'necessity is something that exists in the mind, not in objects' (T, 165), a conclusion which he needs, to support his general thesis that the operations of the mind are the foundations of science, and the science of man, therefore, the fundamental science. If, on the other hand, 'necessarily' (in the assertion, 'P necessarily thinks of E when he encounters C') means 'something more than' constant conjunction, the problem of explaining in what this 'something more' consists will still remain with us; our original philosophical problem breaks out again, in an unmitigated form, within 'the science of man'. Psychology does nothing to 'dissolve' it.

And new problems arise. We are to suppose that the constant conjunction of C with E is the cause of the mind's passing from C to E. This must mean that there is a constant conjunction between C being constantly conjoined with E and the mind's passing from C to E. Is there such a conjunction? We scarcely like to say, because we are embarrassed by the vagueness of 'constant'. If we interpret it as 'conjunction on more than one occasion', this will not do; Hume has admitted that one case is sometimes enough, and two cases are sometimes not enough. If we nominate any specified number of cases, the same sort of difficulty would arise; sometimes the number would not suffice, sometimes a smaller number would suffice. In a 'mature person', Hume has suggested, one case 'properly considered' is all we need. But if this means that 'constant conjunction' can be interpreted as 'single conjunction properly considered', it is presumably the 'proper consideration' which makes the difference—a conclusion which plays havoc with Hume's 'habitual' theory of causal inference. And it is quite impossible to maintain that a single instance is always sufficient.

Indeed, Hume's analysis, at this point, is insufficiently psychological; if the question is—'under what circumstances do we *expect* E?'—no non-psychological answer (like 'constant conjunction') will suffice. What we expect depends, to a very large extent, on what we want. Suppose, to take a trivial example, we have suspiciously and unwillingly eaten a strange food and later suffer from indigestion. We shall naturally designate that food as the cause of our troubles. But it will take a great many cases before we are convinced that our favourite wine is the malignant agent. Considered as a psychological analysis of expectation, Hume's analysis places undue stress on constant conjunction, as distinct from such factors as the nature of our demands. At this point, his methodological requirements interfere with his psychology quite as seriously as his psychology disturbs his methodology.

There is one further difficulty, which is not, however, internal to his analysis of causality; it consists in the incompatibility of that analysis with his subsequent account of personal identity. Throughout Hume's causal theory, he assumes a self over and above the order of our perceptions. Necessity is defined as 'a connexion which *we feel* in the mind', 'a determination to carry *our* thoughts from one object to another', a determination 'to which *the mind* is carried by habit'. It is not enough to say that there is first of all the impression C, then the impression of necessity N, then a vivid idea of E, because, for one thing, there would then be a simple sequence of perceptions and no way of apprehending, or supposing, a connexion *between* C and E, and, for another thing, Hume wants to explain the *origin* of N. This he can only do by assuming the persistence of a mind which can be affected by the occurrence, on quite distinct occasions, of a C followed by an E. And when he goes on to describe the mind's propensity 'to spread itself on external objects and to conjoin with them any internal impressions which they occasion', he assumes that we can distinguish three things—'external' objects, 'internal' impressions, and a mind to which this externality and internality are relative, and which can confuse one with the other.

A similar assumption runs through the whole of Hume's psychological positivism. Thus his criticism of substance, to which we have already referred, supposes that we confuse between two distinct experiences—the experience of a genuine identity, and the experience of changing, but closely resembling, qualities. 'When we gradually follow an object in its successive changes, the smooth progress of the thought makes us ascribe an identity to the succession; because 'tis by a similar act of the mind we consider an unchangeable object' (T, 220). Now, if all that happens is that a succession of impressions which are very much alike follow one another, the 'confusion' could not arise; it must be supposed that a mind stands over the impressions and fails to notice that they differ slightly from one another. In the same way, in order to account for our belief in the existence of external objects, Hume has to evoke a 'general rule' that 'whatever ideas place the mind in the same disposition are very apt to be confounded' (T, 203). Once again, a mere sequence of perceptions will not serve; ideas cannot confound themselves; if there is to be a confounding there must be someone who is confused.

Exactly, then, as Hume's analysis of 'necessity' rests on the assumption that 'necessity' in 'P is necessitated to think of E' requires no analysis, so his analyses of identity in diversity and of independent existence assume that we are directly acquainted with an independently existing self, which maintains its identity beneath the diversity of its perceptions. But whereas Hume never undertakes an analysis of mental necessity he does try to give an account of personal identity; and in the process he gradually becomes aware that the philosophical problems from which he thought he had freed himself break out again within 'the science of man'.

He begins in a spirit of complete confidence. 'The intellectual world', he says, 'tho' involv'd in infinite obscurities, is not perplexed with any such contradictions, as those we have discovered in the natural' (T, 232). We must first get rid of metaphysics—in this case, the theory of a permanent self. His positivist technique is called into play. If we have an idea of the self as an entity, that idea must derive from an impression. But the self cannot be any single impression, since all impressions are supposed to 'have a reference to' it; and no impression can be simple and invariable, as is the self of the metaphysicians. The self, then, we do not encounter in experience; what do we there discover? 'When I enter most intimately into what I call myself, I always stumble on some particular perception or other, of heat or cold, light or shade, love or hatred, pain or pleasure' (T, 252). Thus we can no more describe 'the nature of' personal identity than we could 'the nature of' necessity. The real problem is a psychological one: 'what gives us so great a propension to ascribe an identity to these successive perceptions?' (T, 253).

Two senses of 'personal identity', Hume suggests, must be distinguished—personal identity 'as it regards our thought or imagination' and 'as it regards our passions or the concern we take in ourselves' (T, 253). Only the first of these, he says, is 'his present subject'. This is an important remark; Hume sees that it would be ridiculous to suppose that when we talk, for example, of 'self-love', we mean 'love of all our perceptions' (which would include other people). He will later suggest that we have an 'idea, or rather impression of ourselves' (T, 317); by 'ourselves' he means 'that individual person of whose actions and sentiments each of us is intimately conscious' (T, 286). But the fact remains that he never brings the two sorts of personal identity into relation with one another; and he is quite prepared to speak of 'light or shade, love or hatred', as if our 'thoughts' and our 'passions' were on exactly the same footing.

At first, he approaches his main question indirectly; he will give a general account of the identity attaching to 'plants and animals', and from that, he considers, a special account of personal identity will be found to follow, as a particular application. His general theory of 'animal' identity, as is only natural, is a development of his general theory of identity in diversity. We have an idea of perfect identity: 'a distinct idea of an object, that remains unchangeable through a supposed variation of time'; we also have an idea of diversity, under which we include the case of 'several distinct ideas existing together and connected by a close relation'. But although identity and diversity are quite distinct, in those cases where the relation is a close one they are constantly 'confounded with one another'. 'The relation', Hume continues, 'facilitates the transition of the mind from one object to another, and renders its passage as smooth as if it contemplated one continu'd object' (T, 254). Thus 'the mind' is led to suppose that the perceptions are somehow linked together by a genuinely identical entity; we 'run into the notion of a soul, and self, and substance, to disguise the variation'. This happens even when the 'close relation' between the perceptions consists in nothing more than resemblance, but the tendency is much stronger when, as in the case of 'animal' identity, they are causally linked with one another, or conspire to a common end.

The fiction of personal identity must arise in the same sort of way; it is only as a special concession—'lest this [the preceding] argument should not convince the reader'—that Hume embarks upon a particular consideration of it. But it soon becomes clear that personal identity presents him with very special problems; or, more accurately, that it makes uncomfortably prominent those difficulties in his psychological positivism which he has so far managed to conceal. 'Every distinct perception', he says, 'which enters into the composition of the mind, is a distinct existence, and is different, and distinguishable, and separable from every other perception, either contemporary or successive. But, as, notwithstanding this distinction and separability, we suppose the whole train of perceptions to be united by identity, a question naturally arises concerning this relation of identity;

whether it be something that really binds our several perceptions together, or only associates their ideas in the imagination. That is, in other words, whether in pronouncing concerning the identity of a person, we observe some real bond among his perceptions, or only feel one among the ideas we form of them' (T, 259).

Now, it may in the first place be pointed out that we do not in fact 'suppose the whole train of perceptions to be united by identity'. We do not ordinarily believe that hot and cold, love and hate, light and shade all form part of a single continuous entity. The love and the anger are *us*—we hate or love; the light and shade are perceived by us, but are not part of us; sometimes we *are* hot and cold, sometimes we *are aware of* heat and cold. Thus the problem of personal identity, in Hume's version of it, is wrongly stated; the real question is why, in Hume's terminology, certain of our 'perceptions' are taken to be 'ourselves' and others to be 'our objects'. This problem he does not attempt to solve; indeed, if all our perceptions are united by resemblance and causality, and these relations are all that is necessary to create a fiction of identity, the problem is an insoluble one.

Secondly, Hume simplifies his problem by asking whether in speaking of 'a person' 'we perceive some real bond among his perceptions or only feel one among the ideas we form of them'. Here it is assumed that we begin from a comparison between '*his* perceptions' and 'the ideas *we* form of them'. But, on Hume's showing, we start from perceptions which are all of them equally *ours*; there is no way of distinguishing certain of them as perceptions of someone else's perceptions, and certainly no method of comparing them with the other person's perceptions themselves.

This curious, sudden, and totally unjustifiable shift from the problem of *our* identity to the problem of other people's identity no doubt arises out of the uncomfortable question which Hume finds himself asking: 'whether it [identity] be something that really binds our several perceptions together, or only associates their ideas in the imagination.' For, on the face of it, if identity associates ideas in the imagination, then it really does bind our perceptions together. Confronted with the general problem of identity he could ask: is there really identity beneath diversity or do we construct identity as a fiction? But there are obvious awkwardnesses in asking: is there really identity beneath *our* diversity or do *we* construct the illusion of identity? Hence, Hume shifts to another question: are the perceptions of *other people* really united or do we unite them by a fiction? But then his illicit representationalism reaches too outrageous a point.

The fundamental problem, however, is what it is which confuses succession with identity; and, equally, what it is which comes to recognize that succession *has been* confused with identity. In Hume's effort to cope with this problem, new faculties emerge, under old names. In particular, 'the understanding' displays its Protean qualities. 'The understanding', writes Hume, 'never observes any real connexion among objects (T, 259); from this we are to deduce that identity is the work of 'the imagination'. But the understanding Hume officially defines as 'the general and more established properties of the imagination' (T, 267); on that showing, it is precisely what does take our perceptions to be connected. Now we are to think of it, instead, as a faculty of pure awareness, which sees perceptions as 'they really are', before the imagination has got to work on them. That there is such a faculty Hume must assume; it must be possible to know that our perceptions are *really* distinct—here, at least, the imagination must be kept at bay. The 'understanding', then, considers perceptions in their pure state and finds that they are not 'really bound'; they are, however, associatively linked, and so 'the imagination' cannot resist uniting them, especially since 'the memory' brings before it past perceptions which are very like those which now confront it. This is pure mythology; and yet without it Hume cannot move a step. For if all that happens is that a series of very similar (or causally linked) perceptions succeed one another, there is no possible way in which this series of itself could generate the fiction of personal identity. Nor, the fiction once generated, could this series ever reveal its fictional character. Both the original fiction and the discovery that it is a fiction are possible only if there is something which is at first misled by, and then, after reconsideration, can discover that it was misled by, a series of similar perceptions.

Thus one is not surprised to find that Hume came to be discontented with his theory of personal identity. 'All my hopes vanish', he wrote in the Appendix to the *Treatise*, 'when I come to explain the principles, that unite our successive perceptions in our thought or consciousness . . . in short, there are two principles, which I cannot render consistent; nor is it in my power to renounce either of them, viz. that all our distinct perceptions are distinct existences, and that the mind never perceives any real connexion among distinct existences' (T, 636). Now, of course, these principles are not, as they stand, inconsistent; but they are together inconsistent with a third 'principle'—that the mind perceives a real connexion among our perceptions. And what Hume is unable to explain is how we could come to believe that there is a real connexion among our perceptions unless there is already a real connexion in existence.

At this point, then, Hume's psychological positivism breaks down. He cannot succeed in replacing the philosophical problem—*how can identity and diversity be reconciled?*—by the psychological problem—*how do we come to believe that what is actually diverse possesses identity?*—because unless diversity and identity can in fact be reconciled the psychological problem is insoluble. We suggested that the reduction of philosophy to psychology is, in fact, no more successful in the case of causality than it is in the case of identity. But only in regard to personal identity does Hume recognize his failure; his two principles, he thinks, cannot be reconciled with the facts of that case; he has no intention of abandoning them as a general method of analysis. Nor does he see quite why he has gone wrong; he still lives in hope that 'further reflection' will enable him to overcome his difficulties. The reflection does not seem to have been successful. Hume's analysis of personal identity plays no part in the *Enquiry*—Hume saw that he could not use it as illustration of his main thesis—but he never admits that it is an insuperable obstacle to his positivist project. That it is such an obstacle, we have tried to show.

CHAPTER V

THE PHENOMENALIST

'PUT shortly, Hume's object is to carry further the negative argument initiated by Berkeley, by showing that what we know is limited to a series of sensations, passions and emotions, together with mental images of them, and that it is groundless to believe in the existence of anything else, even ourselves.' This quotation is from H. A. Prichard's *Knowledge and Perception* (p. 178), but the interpretation it presents is common to the majority of critics and historians. An insular trinity—Locke, Berkeley, Hume— 'British empiricists' all of them, with Hume, in Reid's words, presenting 'the only system to which the theory of ideas leads, a system which is, in all its parts, a necessary consequence of that theory'[1]—that is the picture of British philosophy which, until very recently, we have been invited to condemn or to admire.

Now, however, the accuracy of that picture has been seriously challenged. Kemp Smith has directed massive broadsides against the 'Reid-Green' interpretation of Hume, and these are beginning to have some effect upon the historians of philosophy. Russell, it is true, in his *History of Western Philosophy* still writes that 'he developed to its logical conclusion the empirical philosophy of Locke and Berkeley, and by making it self-consistent, made it incredible' (p. 685); and the influence of Russell's book will no doubt help to perpetuate the older view. But other writers, such as A. D. Woozley, push Kemp Smith's radical interpretation to a more extreme point. 'Hume', writes Woozley, 'could have scrapped Part I entire and have substituted almost any other analysis of the objects of cognition without having to alter in essentials any of the arguments that follow. What was vital to his main theories was that our experience should be made up of a sequence of discrete

---

[1] *Essays on the Intellectual Powers of Man*, Essay IV, Chapter iii.

particulars, but what the mental or material status of those particulars was, was not of much account.'[1]

But 'discrete particulars', most assuredly, will not serve, if Hume's 'main theories' are those which he particularly emphasized. That what we immediately perceive is 'mental' is a doctrine which Hume needs for his defence of the moral sciences, for his special variety of positivism, and (up to a point) for his scepticism, to say nothing of his associationist intentions. Yet the point Woozley is over-emphasizing is an important one: many (though most certainly not all) of Hume's theories are largely independent of the theory of ideas. Hume's criticism of the view that induction is a species of implication, to take only one case, can be restated in a form which is largely independent of Hume's theory of perception. One must certainly reject the view, ossified in Chambers's *Cyclopedia of Literature* (1844), that 'the leading doctrine of Hume is that all the objects of our knowledge are divided into two classes—impressions and ideas'; one must certainly draw attention to the great importance, in Hume's theory, of the assumption that 'discrete particulars' are the constituents of our experience (a fact that Green, for one, fully recognized). But it is still necessary to insist upon the merits of the Reid-Green criticism of Hume, still necessary to insist on the importance of the 'theory of ideas' in Hume's philosophy, for all that the destruction of that theory does not carry with it, as an inevitable consequence, a complete 'answer to Hume'.

The traditional view, however, made use of an historical assumption, a very natural one, which is quite erroneous: the assumption that Hume's object was, in Prichard's words, 'to carry further' the philosophy of Berkeley. Green's collaborator, Grose, summed up the historical situation thus: 'The *Treatise* from beginning to end is the work of a solitary Scotchman, who has devoted himself to the critical study of Locke and Berkeley. That he lived for three years in France, was an accident which has left no trace either in the tone or in the matter of his book.'[2] On this point, Dr Johnson showed more than his usual

---

[1] Introduction to his edition of Reid's *Essays*, p. xii.
[2] 'History of the Editions' (p. 40) in G.G., III.

perspicacity: 'Why, Sir, his style is not English; the structure of his sentences is French.'[1] And the writings of Laird and Kemp Smith should by now have made the fact sufficiently notorious that Hume's 'matter', as well as his 'tone', was infected by French influence; his borrowings from Malebranche and Pierre Bayle were conspicuous and substantial. It is still too often assumed, however, that Hume was a devoted student of Berkeley. Of course, there is at least one matter—his rejection of abstract ideas—on which Hume owed a great deal to Berkeley; and at other times Berkeley's philosophy was no doubt before his mind. The fact remains that he does not take Berkeley's central argument at all seriously.

Beattie drew attention to the fundamental point of difference: Hume does not try to maintain that his theory 'differs not from that of the rest of mankind'[2]—which was Berkeley's constant refrain. A recent commentator, in the course of his severe criticism of Hume's motives, asserts that if Hume had been genuinely interested in science 'he would have followed Berkeley's thorough-going realism'; he did not do so, according to this critic, only because 'subjectivism is universally shocking', so that Hume was anxious to employ 'its great publicity value.'[3] This complaint would certainly have astonished Berkeley's contemporaries and, very clearly, would have staggered Hume himself. No one in his own time detected Berkeley's 'realism'. 'It is pleasant to observe', says Reid, 'the fruitless pains which Bishop Berkeley takes to show that his system of the non-existence of the world did not contradict the sentiments of the vulgar';[4] Berkeley's protestations no one took with any seriousness. Hume called Berkeley a 'sceptic'. No doubt, he took a mischievous delight in thus retorting upon Berkeley an epithet he so often directed against others, but, still, this view was reasonably representative of contemporary opinion. It certainly never occurred to Dr Johnson that Berkeley was a 'realist', although he conceded that he was 'a man of fine imagination'. Had Hume been content to startle, he needed to

[1] Boswell's *Life* (Everyman edition: Vol. i, p. 272).
[2] *Essay on Truth*, p. 282.   [3] J. H. Randall, in *Freedom and Experience*, p. 299.
[4] *Op. cit.*, Essay VI, Ch. iv.

follow Berkeley, not to reject him. As it is, he uses Berkeley as a horrible example of what rational argument can lead to. It is a striking fact that Hume does not even bother to argue against Berkeley, at points where he disagrees with him. Berkeley, for example, said that we know our mind as an agency, even although we do not know it as an idea: this suggestion Hume does not trouble himself to mention, even when he is specifically discussing our knowledge of our own mind. In the *Enquiry*, it is true, he criticizes Berkeley's view that we are directly acquainted with causal 'power', in the form of our own activity, but even this doctrine Hume did not so much as mention until he came to write the Appendix to the *Treatise*. Another passage in the Appendix is significant. Hume there draws attention to an error in the *Treatise*; he had said that we estimate distance by calculating from 'the angles which the rays of light flowing from the bodies make with each other'. ''Tis certain', he now writes, 'that these angles are not known to the mind, and consequently can never discover the distance' (T, 636). Hume's 'error' derives from Malebranche;[1] a close student of Berkeley could not have failed to notice the arguments he directed against this theory of vision, the very arguments which Hume adopts in the Appendix, but apparently knew nothing of when he was writing the main body of the *Treatise*.

Hume, it would appear, composed the *Treatise* with Malebranche and Bayle, along with Locke and Hutcheson, in the forefront of his mind; Berkeley, one suspects, had been left behind in England, and was not read again until the first two books of the *Treatise* had been published. But even if the works of Berkeley were not physically remote, the whole spirit of his enterprise was alien to Hume. In many ways, Berkeley had the more philosophical mind; he was prepared to work out a hypothesis in detail, with a real concern for consistency— Hume, in contrast, was a philosophical puppy-dog, picking up and worrying one problem after another, always leaving

[1] *Recherche*, 1, 69 (Bk I, Ch. x). This is the crucial point on which Berkeley refused to follow Malebranche's theory of vision, to which he was otherwise much indebted.

his teeth-marks in it, but casting it aside when it threatened to become wearisome. And, of course, Berkeley's spiritualism was distasteful; Hume was ready to criticize Newtonianism in the interests of 'the science of man', but not in order to substitute for it a theological scheme of things.

Malebranche, odd as that may seem, was very much more to Hume's taste. Certainly, Malebranche saw all things in God, but God, Hume thought, he could excise: 'we are got into fairyland, long ere we have reached the last steps of our theory' (E, 72). And what was left suited Hume admirably. Every cause (with none of Berkeley's exceptions) is experienced as a constant conjunction, never as an agency; we do not know the substance of the soul, but only 'ce que nous sentons se passer en nous';[1] our knowledge of external bodies is an act of faith, not an inference; there are animal spirits, to the vagaries of which our errors can be traced. At point after point Hume found in Malebranche something he could turn to his purposes, without being obliged to depart too far from the atmosphere of Locke's *Essay*, with all its negligent concessions. He does not conceal his high opinion of what he calls 'the glory of Malebranche' (E, 7); he goes so far, indeed, as to ascribe to him 'that abstract theory of morals, which was later adopted by Cudworth, Clarke and others'.[2] Probably he thought, as Reid did, that 'Bishop Berkeley's arguments are found in him [Malebranche] in their full force':[3] hence Berkeley (on most matters) could be safely neglected.

Nevertheless, we suggested, there is something to be said for the traditional view that Hume carried to a final conclusion the

[1] *Recherche*, III, 2, 8.

[2] E, 197. Malebranche and Cudworth are close to one another at many points; if we look merely at dates of publication (*Recherche*, 1675, *True Intellectual System*, 1678), we might think that Hume's historical excursion was an accurate description of the facts. But in fact the *True Intellectual System* was completed by 1671, and Cudworth's 'rational ethics' was formulated as early as 1644 (see my *Ralph Cudworth*). If, then, there were any indebtedness in the case, Malebranche would be the borrower, but the fact that both men were Cartesian Platonists would sufficiently explain the points of resemblance between them. As for Clarke—Grotius, Cicero and Cumberland were his masters.

[3] *Op. cit.*, Essay II, Ch. vii.

assumptions of Locke's *Essay*, that, in a way, he out-Berkeleyed Berkeley. The established tradition no doubt has its absurdities, which arouse Kemp Smith to exclamation: 'Hume, who was sceptical—so it was alleged—about almost everything else, has yet been so uncritical as to erect the elaborate body of argument which constitutes the *Treatise* on a foundation which he has not been concerned to examine, and to the unreliability of which he has himself, though all unconsciously, been a chief witness!'[1] Kemp Smith is right in insisting that one cannot properly argue—for it seriously begs the crucial question—that Hume unconsciously produces a *reductio ad absurdum* of Locke's *Essay*; one must not ascribe to Hume one's own definition of absurdity. But, as against Kemp Smith, there is nothing surprising in the fact that Hume, for all his strict scrutiny of assumptions, yet failed sufficiently to examine the theory of ideas.

Notoriously, his exposition of that theory is careless and confused; this is not because the theory was of no concern to him, but because he felt that on this point he need expect no serious criticism. ''Tis universally allowed by philosophers, and is besides pretty obvious of itself, that nothing is ever really present with the mind but its perceptions, or impressions and ideas, and that external objects become known to us only by those perceptions they occasion' (T, 67). Bayle had made precisely the same point. 'None among good philosophers', he wrote, 'now doubt that the sceptics are right to maintain that the qualities of bodies which strike our senses are only mere appearances'.[2] Descartes, Locke, Berkeley, Malebranche, Hutcheson, all taught the same lesson; they disagreed about the precise manner in which material objects were related to perceptions, but did not question that the immediate objects of mind are perceptions.

But was phenomenalism the direction in which Hume developed the theory of ideas? Our answer to this question will naturally depend on what we mean by phenomenalism. Laird's definition will serve as a starting-point: 'phenomenalism', he says, 'is the doctrine that all our knowledge, all our belief, and

[1] *Philosophy of David Hume*, p. 4. [2] *Dictionary*, art. *Pyrrho* (Note B).

all our conjectures begin and end with appearances; that we cannot go behind or beyond these; and that we should not try to do so.'[1] In this sense of the word, I should say, Hume was not, in the end, a phenomenalist, was indeed an anti-phenomenalist; for he regarded phenomenalism as a variety of 'excessive scepticism', the sort of scepticism which no one can persistently maintain. We cannot help, whether we like it or not, going beyond 'appearances'. He *was* a phenomenalist, however, in a narrower sense—he argued that we could not *know* anything but 'perceptions', in that restricted sense of 'know' in which it means 'be certain of, without any risk of error', nor can we even infer by any sort of 'probable reasoning' that anything else exists. So long as he restricts himself to the traditional methods of philosophers, he speaks as a phenomenalist; but this, in his eyes, is part of the evidence that these methods will not suffice.

The traditional view ascribes to Hume Berkeley's philosophy without God and the Self; but *in his actual beliefs* he is much closer to Locke than he is to Berkeley. If we ask what Hume believed, what view he committed himself to in his scientific work, the answer is that he believed in the existence both of material objects *and* of perceptions, and thought that perceptions were ' appearances of' material objects. 'No man, who reflects, ever doubted', he says, 'that the existences, which we consider, when we say, *this house* and *that tree*, are nothing but perceptions in the mind and fleeting copies or representations of other existences, which remain uniform and independent' (E, 152). Admittedly he goes on to suggest, in a manner we shall examine in a subsequent chapter, that these views, even though they are 'the obvious dictates of the reason', cannot be defended against the equally rational arguments of the sceptic—in which company Berkeley is included. The fact remains that something like Lockianism must be true even though it is not rationally defensible; Berkeley's subjectivism 'produces no conviction' (E, 155n), the vulgar view that our perceptions are the external objects cannot stand up to the slightest critical examination. Prichard complains that 'there is in Hume just as

[1] *Hume's Philosophy of Human Nature*, p. 25.

much unjustified transition from objects to ideas and *vice versa* as there is in Locke'.[1] Hume would reply that the transition although 'unjustified'—if all justification has to be rational—was nevertheless inevitable.

Now, this, to many philosophers, would be the *reductio ad absurdum* of the theory of ideas; if we cannot know, or rationally infer, that anything but ideas exist, and yet must at the same time believe that there are material objects, this 'inconsistency' shows that the theory of ideas must be abandoned. Hume's attitude is very different. The theory of ideas, he assumes, is established; no one can doubt that we are directly aware only of 'perceptions'; here is a point which his scepticism does not touch. It was a point in the favour of that theory, not an argument against it, that it shows reason to be impotent in all matters of fact. If the theory of ideas had not already been worked out, Hume would have had to invent it. As it was, the work was done for him: he had a foundation on which his scepticism, his psychological positivism, his insistence on the primacy of the moral sciences, could immediately be erected. Malebranche, for example, had already shown that the question —'How can we *prove* that bodies exist?'—is unanswerable; that part of Hume's work was done; he need only add that we should, for that question, substitute the *psychological* problem: 'How do we come to believe that bodies exist?'

We cannot answer Hume, then, by arguing that the theory of ideas is 'untenable', if all we mean by this is that it provides us with no *ground* for believing in the existence of independent things; Hume would accept our 'refutation' with ironic gratitude, as he did Reid's.[2] If, on the other hand, we can show either that we are not immediately acquainted with 'perceptions', or that Hume cannot, on his initial assumptions, account for the *origin* of our belief in material objects, we have frustrated some at least of Hume's major intentions, although others of them depend rather on the assumption of 'discrete particulars' than on the supposed 'mentality' of such particulars. Those who persist in upholding the theory of ideas must either argue that there are ways in which 'the world of sense' can be

---

[1] *Knowledge and Perception*, p. 178.   [2] *Letters*, 1, 375.

derived from perceptions,[1] or else be prepared to accept beliefs to which our experience lends no support. But those who reject the theory of ideas may answer Hume in a different fashion.

So important a part does this theory play in Hume's philosophy, so intimately is it entwined with his special views on a variety of subjects (and in particular with the associationism and the scepticism which are to be our concern in subsequent chapters) that, for the moment, we must be content to explore its implications in one area only: Hume's attempt to work out a phenomenalist 'psychology of knowledge' which would give an account of the traditional 'mental acts'—thinking, perceiving, remembering, imagining, believing—without making any reference to independent existence, or to anything except 'perceptions'. So far he must be a phenomenalist. To pass beyond 'perceptions' is to leave knowledge for conjectures; if the science of man is to be judged superior to physical science it must be able to complete its work—which includes the analysis of those 'mental acts' upon which every other science depends—without venturing beyond the security of our immediate perceptions. And his attempt to develop this view, more than anything else, leads Hume in the direction of a phenomenalist theory of reality, even though that is a view in which he does not, and cannot, rest content.

Hume begins with two classes of perceptions—impressions and ideas. 'Impressions' he describes in the *Treatise* as 'striking upon the mind', although he goes on to say—here distinguishing his position from that of writers like Malebranche[2]—that he does not, in using the word 'impression', intend to refer to 'the manner in which our lively perceptions are produced in the mind' but simply to the perceptions themselves. At the opening of the *Enquiry* he was somewhat more careful in his manner of expression. There is no more talk of 'striking upon the mind'; impressions are described, simply, as a species of perception.

---

[1] 'Derived' in its broadest sense, in which it would include deduced from, constructed out of, 'reasonably inferred from' etc. For examples of such derivations see the works of Russell, e.g. his *History of Western Philosophy*, p. 699, or his *Human Knowledge, passim.* But Russell now grants that we need at least one auxiliary principle which is neither a perception nor derived from perceptions. [2] cf. Laird, *Hume's Philosophy*, p. 26.

This does not mean that Hume ever doubted that impressions *were* produced in the mind by some sort of physiological mechanism ('the examination of our sensations', he says, 'belongs more to anatomists and natural philosophers than to moral' (T, 8)). He came to recognize, however, that he must not begin by assuming that there are either 'minds' or 'material objects'.

Neither in the *Enquiry* nor in the *Treatise* does Hume devote much attention to the distinction between ideas and impressions—even although it was to be used with such confidence as the scourge of metaphysicians and theologians. There is a reason for this casualness and brevity: Hume was introducing a new terminology rather than a new doctrine. 'All good philosophers', he thought, agreed that we are directly acquainted with perceptions; they also agreed that perceptions fall into two classes, whether these were called sensations and images, or ideas and impressions. (Hartley is quite as casual, on this matter, as Hume, and for precisely the same reason.) The criteria by which Hume distinguishes the two types of perception had no more novelty in them.[1] An impression is more lively than an idea; and ideas are copies of impressions. All this, except the terminology, was so familiar that Hume could mention, merely as a curiosity, that there were sometimes ideas which did not seem to copy any impression. The 'effrontery', as Prichard calls it, with which he makes this negligent concession is a testimony to what he takes to be the firmly-established character of his main position; but it illustrates, also, that insensitivity to consistency which Hume shares with Locke.

There is a similar casualness in Hume's account of memory and imagination. The mode of distinction is very similar. Ideas of memory are more vivid than ideas of imagination; and they retain, whereas imagination modifies, the original order of our experiences. These were quite familiar points of distinction; and Hume lightly admits that ideas of memory are not *always* more vivid than ideas of imagination. More than

[1] cf. Laird, *op. cit.*, pp. 32-3, for references to Descartes, Malebranche, and Berkeley.

this, he makes an admission which is really fatal: 'Tho' it be a peculiar property of the memory to preserve the original order and position of its ideas, while the imagination transposes and changes them, as it pleases; yet this difference is not sufficient to distinguish them in their operation, or make us know the one from the other; it being impossible to recall the past impressions, in order to compare them with our present ideas, and see whether their arrangement be exactly similar' (T, 85). Hume finds this admission useful, as a stage in the development of his theory of belief. We believe our memory (to speak crudely); if that belief can be reduced merely to the *vivacity* of certain of our ideas, this will help to establish the general thesis that belief of every kind can be defined in terms of vivacity. (At this stage in his argument, Hume is intent upon establishing that all our beliefs are of the same sort; later, when he wants to anchor our 'reliable' beliefs more firmly to impressions, this freeing of memory from its relation to the past—this loss of a reliable 'copy'—is distinctly inconvenient.)

Hume is clearly right: if 'all our impressions are perishing existences and appear as such', it is impossible to recall them; what is recalled must *ex hypothesi* be an idea. But he never realizes the full implications of this admission. Taken seriously, it would destroy his positivist method. There is now no way of discovering whether a supposed idea in fact derives from an impression; the empirical test can never, in principle, be employed, because it demands that we recall our impressions, which it is never possible to do. An uneasy conscience on points such as these probably accounts for the change which gradually comes over Hume's theory, as a result of which ideas of memory are transformed into impressions. On this matter (and this is no accident, or fit of carelessness) Hume's inconsistencies reach epic proportions; within a few pages of the *Treatise* he describes ideas of the memory as 'equivalent to impressions' (T, 82), speaks of 'an impression of the memory' (T, 84), contemplates 'a repetition of that impression in the memory' (T, 86), and yet never ceases to emphasize that memory presents us with ideas (T, 85). Unless memory presents us with actual impressions, Hume's theory of belief collapses;

and yet, if it does, impressions are no longer 'original existences', with the comforting solidity and actuality that phrase suggests. And also, if both remembering and 'feeling' (observation) consist in our having impressions, Hume cannot possibly explain in the language of perceptions how one can be distinguished from the other or—if he was prepared to argue that they are in fact identical—how anyone ever came to believe that certain of our perceptions have a special relation to the past, that they are 'remembered'.

Suppose we were to say, simply, that the difference is one of vivacity, that 'ideas of the memory' are so vivid that we do not know quite whether to class them with impressions or with ideas —would this suffice for the purposes of Hume's theory? Sometimes he seems to be content with this conclusion: it comports with this theory of sympathy, for example, that 'the different degrees of force and vivacity' should be 'the only particulars' which distinguish impressions from ideas (T, 319). And yet, at other times, he distinguishes impressions from ideas, when 'these only particulars' cannot be the ground of differentiation. He admits, for example, that ideas of the imagination are sometimes more vivid than ideas of the memory—an assertion which is a contradiction in terms, if 'ideas of the imagination' are only distinguishable from 'ideas of the memory' by their lesser vividness. It is unnecessary, at this stage in Hume-criticism, to labour the point. But there is one passage, not very well known, which particularly illustrates the straits to which Hume is driven. He is considering what appears to be an exception to his theory of belief. 'Suppose', he says, 'I form at present an idea, of which I have forgot the correspondent impression, I am able to conclude from this idea that such an impression did once exist: and as this conclusion is attended with belief, it may be ask'd, from whence are the qualities of force and vivacity derived, which constitute this belief?' He answers: 'from the present idea.' 'For', he says, 'as this idea is not here consider'd as the representation of any absent object, but as a real perception in the mind, of which we are intimately conscious, it must be able to bestow on whatever is related to it the same quality, call it firmness, or solidity, or force, or vivacity, with which the mind reflects on it, and is assur'd of its present existence. The idea here supplies the place of an impression, and is entirely the same, so far as regards our present purpose' (T, 105-6). Thus, we can know that a perception is an 'idea' even though

(1) We do not know it as representing an impression.

(2) We do not know it as subsequent to an impression.

(3) It is quite as vivid as an impression.

(4) It gives rise to beliefs in the same way as an impression.

Hume relies on the fact that, as he puts it, 'every one of himself will readily perceive the distinction betwixt feeling and thinking'; he fails seriously to ask himself the crucial question—*could* we make this distinction if we were acquainted with nothing but perceptions?

In ordinary life, we do not distinguish the so-called 'acts of mind' by any sort of introspective analysis, or, at least, we do not regard any such analysis as decisive. Suppose, as quite often happens, we discover that we are 'only imagining' what we thought we were perceiving, or suppose we wish to dispute someone else's claim that he remembers what, we say, he only imagines. Such discoveries and such disputes are, on Hume's view, quite unintelligible. Every perception is what it is known as being; hence a perception cannot 'really' be more vivid than it appears to be. It makes no sense to say that we were 'really' imagining what we thought we were perceiving, that one of our vivid perceptions was 'really faint'. And if someone tells us he is 'remembering', there is no way of disputing his assertion: he knows, and he alone can know, whether he is having a vivid idea—and that is the decisive fact.

At least, on Hume's theory it is decisive; in practice, of course, it is nothing of the kind. We may assert with any degree of vigour and no intention of lying that we are remembering a particular event, but if it can be shown that we were not in a position to observe it (were not alive or were not there), this settles the matter. It will immediately follow that we are not remembering but are only imagining. We may tell the psychiatrist that we most vividly apprehend the presence of a tiger in the room; but we do not *perceive* it if it is not there.

This is the sort of consideration which leads Hume to admit that an 'idea' is not always faint; a consistent phenomenalist would have to abandon such concessions to ordinary usage, would have to say, simply, that our perceptions fall into various classes (distinguishable by their degree of vivacity) and that it is meaningless to suggest that a perception 'really ought' to fall into a class other than the one to which we allocate it.

Such a phenomenalist could not properly describe imagining as less solid, less reliable (in any objective sense) than remembering or perceiving; and Hume's theory of belief at first leads him in this direction—our perceptions, he argues, differ only in vivacity, not in 'reality'. 'Reality', indeed, is nothing but our name for a particular organization of vivid perceptions. This is the side of Hume's theory which inclines us to label him as a phenomenalist. It is worked out in most detail in the earlier sections of the *Treatise* but is a disturbing undercurrent throughout the whole book, even though, as we have already seen, his developed theory of 'belief' by no means identifies it with a 'vivid idea'.

If we were asked to define a belief, our definition might well include a reference to 'existence'; to 'believe', we might say, is to take something to exist. If we are exponents of the theory of ideas, we might add that by 'existence' we mean 'external' existence. Thus, for example, 'believing in God' would mean 'believing that God exists' as distinct from 'having an idea of God'. But this account of 'belief' obviously will not do, if we are to give an account of 'acts of mind' which does not involve any 'conjectures' about the independently existent. So Hume argues that neither by reference to 'existence' nor to 'external existence' can a 'belief' be distinguished from any other perception.

'Whatever we conceive', he says, 'we conceive to be existent.' 'Whoever opposes this', he argues, 'must necessarily point out that distinct impression, from which the idea of entity is deriv'd, and must prove, that this impression is inseparable from every perception we believe to be existent. This we may without hesitation conclude to be impossible' (T, 67). Now, of course, Hume is right in denying that 'existence' is an 'idea' (that it is parallel to 'cat' or 'red'); and there is no room in his official logic for anything which is not a specific idea. But we have already observed that he does not himself adhere to his own doctrine. In his account of contrariety, especially, he finds himself obliged to talk about 'the idea of existence'. A passage in the *Enquiry* brings out his difficulties very clearly. 'That Caesar, or the angel Gabriel, or any being never existed', he says, 'may be a false proposition, but still is perfectly conceivable, and implies no contradiction' (E, 164). But if to conceive a thing is to conceive it as existing, then it *would* 'imply a contradiction' to conceive the non-existence of Gabriel. If, as he says, the judgment 'Gabriel is' contains only the single idea 'Gabriel', what different 'idea' does 'Gabriel is not' contain? And why are we not content to say 'Gabriel', what point is there in adding 'is'?

Hume has, in fact, confused two very different assertions:

1. 'To think of a thing is to think of it as it would be if it existed.'

2. 'To think of a thing is to think that it exists.'

Or as we might put it,

1. 'Whatever we think of has the *form* of a fact.'

2. 'Whatever we think of we *take to be* a fact.'

His logic, as we said, leaves no room for expressions like 'is' which do not refer to 'distinct ideas'; indeed, as we previously tried to show, every logical constant, and therefore the whole notion of form, is officially expelled from Hume's logic. In consequence, he is left with no way of distinguishing between 'having the *form* of a fact' and 'being a fact'.

Furthermore, 'thinking that Gabriel exists' has a meaning only if we can distinguish between 'the existence' of a thing and our thinking of that thing; and in his account of external existence Hume at first denies (quite in the phenomenalist manner) that 'existence' can mean anything else but 'being perceived'. 'Nothing is ever present to the mind but perceptions', he writes, ' . . . 'tis impossible for us so much as to conceive or form an idea of anything specifically different from ideas and impressions . . . let us chase our imagination to the heavens, or to the utmost limits of the universe: we never really advance a step beyond ourselves, nor can conceive any kind of existence, but those perceptions, which have appeared in that narrow compass' (T, 67). This is high eloquence; taken at its face value it would mean that 'existence' is just another word for 'perception', and 'non-existence' not a word for anything (although why we should then repine at our 'narrow compass' remains a mystery). But we must ignore the rhetoric and concentrate on the phrase '*specifically* different from ideas'. For Hume goes on to admit that we can form a 'relative idea' of objects by attributing to our perceptions 'different relations, connexions and durations'. We cannot think of anything except as being a perception of some sort, but we can suppose that certain of our perceptions are systematically inter-connected.

These 'inter-connected perceptions', it is now argued, form the 'real world'; Hume's theory of belief, in its first version, leads him to a view in accordance with which 'to be real' means to play a certain role in a regular system of perceptions. The constituents of this system are our impressions ('of our memory and the senses') and this provides a clue to the general nature of the system, to the criterion for admission to it. 'The *belief* or *assent*, which always attends the memory and senses, is nothing but the vivacity of those perceptions they present' (T, 86). This is awkwardly expressed, with its suggestion that 'memory' presents perceptions (to *us*, presumably) which are then somehow attended by belief. But what Hume means, I suggest—although he cannot express the matter quite in this way, is that we take to exist (to be real) what we perceive or remember and that the only characteristic peculiar to objects of perception and memory is their greater liveliness. Hence, 'to take as real' must consist in having a vivid perception.

But it is not only impressions which we take to be real; sometimes 'belief' attends an idea. How can this be? At this point, Hume's *second* definition of belief—'a lively idea associated with a present impression' (T, 96)—comes to the fore. A certain amount of slipping backwards and forwards between propositions and ideas smooths the passage to this conclusion. Hume wants to show that the *content* of a belief is identical with the content of what is merely entertained (without being believed); for this purpose he uses propositions like 'Caesar dy'd in his bed'.

But it is clearly a very long way around (even via the theory of testimony) to any 'present impression' with which this proposition is 'associated'; hence he slips into a quite different kind of example—believing that something is going to come to pass (with the help of causal inference)—although the identity of *content* could not in this case with the same facility be demonstrated. He is, I suspect, rather uneasily conscious of his manœuvres; it is at this point that he adds the footnote in which 'judgments' are identified with 'ideas'. We are to suppose that what is true of ideas must be true of judgments and vice versa. In every case, therefore, our 'beliefs' must have the same content as our fancies, and in every case they must be linked with our present impressions.

Yet the fact is that, as was pointed out in an earlier chapter, he now substantially abandons the pretence of giving a general theory of belief, admitting, for example, that 'education' produces in us 'beliefs' which are not associated with impressions. His curious behaviour at this point arises out of the fact that he is trying to impose upon a psychological theory of belief the responsibility of functioning as a general account of 'reality'; as so often happens, psychology as well as logic suffers in consequence. The question he really has before him is not: 'What is believing?' but rather this: 'Granted that our impressions are "real", what else is "real"?' And his answer is that we take as 'real' whatever is linked by causal inferences with our impressions, an answer which is, however, disguised as a definition of 'belief'.

We construct a system, at first including only our present and past impressions—'and every particular of that system we are pleased to call a reality'. To this system the mind adds another connected by 'custom, or, if you will, the relation of cause and effect', and this system 'it likewise dignifies with the title of *realities*' (T, 108). The language should be noted: this is the climax of Hume's phenomenalism—'we are pleased to call a reality'; the mind 'dignifies with the title of realities'. In other words, we simply choose to give the name 'reality' to a particular set of ideas and impressions. To believe, to take to be real, is to allocate to a place in this system.

One obvious objection is that people take things to be real which are neither impressions nor causally linked with impressions; Hume grants, as we have seen, that education can generate beliefs, and that mere resemblance, as distinct from causality, can have the same effect. These 'beliefs', however, form no part of reality. But why not? The fact is that 'reality', for all Hume's pretence to the contrary, has an honorific sense; 'the mind' which constructs 'reality' is not just any mind (which might be swayed by mere fancies) but the *philosophic* mind. If metaphysicians or enthusiasts try to dignify *their* ideas with the name of 'reality', Hume will protest that *their* beliefs have no 'foundation in experience'. But if an impression is only a lively perception, it is no more of a 'foundation' than any other lively perception, than, for example, the vivid fancies of the enthusiast. So we find Hume shifting to his other criterion: the systems of the metaphysician would be irregular, lacking 'force and settled order'. (There is, it is worth noting, a very similar shift from verification to coherence in recent positivism, arising out of the same difficulty in 'justifying' the primacy of sensory experience.) And, once more, Hume would not be prepared, in every mood, to admit that a preference for regularity is a mere prejudice.

It is instructive to observe what happens in the *Enquiry*. 'Education', with all its embarrassments, disappears; and so does 'the system of the judgment'. And some of Hume's most Lockian expressions take their place. There is 'a kind of pre-established harmony between the course of nature, and the succession of our ideas'. Nature has 'implanted in us an instinct which carries forward the thought in a correspondent course to that which she has established among external objects' (E, 54-55). Such of our 'beliefs' as are causally engendered (the 'beliefs' which constitute 'reality') have a solid foundation in Nature; no less solid foundation will do, if the appeal to 'reality' or 'experience' is to be used as a weapon against superstition and metaphysics.

In the Appendix to the *Treatise*, Hume's theory of belief is already making him uneasy; he reverts to it on four separate occasions and in a way which serves to confirm the interpretation of it which we have suggested. In the first passage (T, 623-7), his *third* theory of belief is predominant; he explicitly pronounces that 'we can never be induc'd to believe any matter of fact, except where its cause or its effect is present to us'. How do beliefs differ from other ideas? We cannot say that belief adds the idea of 'reality' or 'existence' to our perceptions, he argues, because we have 'no abstract idea of existence'. The difference, then, must lie in the 'feeling' or 'sentiment' which attaches to beliefs. This does not mean that a peculiar internal impression ('mental act') accompanies our beliefs; when we examine our beliefs, according to Hume, we find no such impression. The 'feeling' of belief must consist simply in the fact that some of our beliefs are 'firmer' or 'more solid' than others. 'They strike upon us with more force; they are more present to us; the mind has a firmer hold of them and is more actuated and moved by them. It acquiesces in them; and in a manner, fixes and reposes itself on them' (T, 624). This is queer language for a writer to whom beliefs are actually *parts* of our mind. We are not surprised when, in the third of the Appendix passages, Hume confesses that 'I am at a loss for terms to express my meaning' (T, 628). He is certain only that a belief *feels* different from other ideas—although no word, neither 'force' nor 'vivacity' nor 'solidity' nor 'firmness' nor 'steadiness', quite satisfies him as a description of that feeling. 'But its true and proper name is *belief* which is a term that everyone sufficiently understands in common life' (T, 629). This peculiar feeling, according to the fourth of the Appendix passages (T, 631), does not attach to 'poetical enthusiasm' but only to 'serious conviction'. And he continues thus: 'we observe, that the vigour of conception, which fictions receive from poetry and eloquence, is a circumstance merely accidental, of which every idea is equally susceptible, and that such fictions are connected with nothing that is real.' Thus, after all, 'reality' has the final word; a serious conviction (illicitly identified with 'justifiable belief') is linked with impressions, and thus with our mode of access to reality.

Why does Hume find it so difficult to find a word for 'the feeling of belief'? What has happened, I suggest, is that he is trying to amalgamate into a single notion 'belief', in the sense of believing, and 'belief', in the sense of what is believed; and no word or expression quite succeeds in amalgamating the two different senses. Hume sees that there is no *single* act of mind called 'believing'; he concludes that what we usually call the 'attitude' of belief, qualifying it in such phrases as 'a strongly-held belief', as distinct from such phrases as 'a false belief', is actually, in a queer sort of way, a characteristic of the belief. This characteristic must be one which does not add to the content of the believed 'idea' (since an idea has the same content after we believe it as it had before we believed it); and it must be transferable—the 'believedness' of an impression can be communicated to associated ideas without the impression itself diminishing in force. No wonder Hume has difficulty in nominating a characteristic which will satisfy these conditions! We find him even asserting that the peculiarity of belief lies in 'the manner of conception', quite as if 'belief' were, after all, an attitude of the believer, as distinct from a property of the believed. Only then, indeed, does his theory light into intelligibility. Suppose, for example, we think of 'belief' as a way of 'being interested in'. If A is interested in B, that interest can be transferred to C, with which B is closely associated, without his interest in B diminishing (transferability); what we are interested in we look closely at (vivacity); what we believe (to turn to the *object* of belief) we regard as 'solid': it resists us, we cannot do what we like with it. But it is not intelligible to suggest that one *idea* is more 'solid' than another, or that ideas can have characters which are not part of their content, or that 'an idea' can be distinguished as 'it' from 'the manner of conceiving *it*'. 'Vivacity' will simply not serve, if we try to substitute it for the independent interests of the believer, and the objectivity of the believed.

In general, this analysis suggests that without a reference to independent existence it is quite impossible to explain why certain of our 'perceptions' are picked out as sensations, or as memories, or as 'images', or as beliefs. Hume could say no more, if he remained faithful to a phenomenalist interpretation of 'mental acts', than that perceptions (whatever leads us to describe them in this way rather than as things) are some-times alike and sometimes different (this is all that 'faint copy' can mean). The question which remains for our consideration is whether 'association' could construct out of this unpromising material the world with which we ordinarily have dealings.

CHAPTER VI

THE ASSOCIATIONIST

THAT Hume himself, even after the completion of the *Treatise*, thought that his associationism was his most notable achievement, he makes abundantly clear in the *Abstract*. 'Thro' this whole book', he writes, 'there are great pretensions to new discoveries in philosophy; but if anything can entitle the author to so glorious a name as that of an *inventor*, 'tis the use he makes of the principle of the association of ideas, which enters into most of his philosophy' (A, 31). Notice the phrase—'the use he makes': Hume does not claim to have invented the theory of association, but only to have discovered a new use for it— although he does, in the *Enquiry*, describe himself as the first who has 'attempted to enumerate or class all the principles of association' (E, 24); a task which, in fact, Aristotle had sought to accomplish.[1]

It is a fact 'too obvious to escape observation' that 'different ideas are connected together' (E, 24); what Hume's predecessors had not observed, he thought, is that these associative connexions are the main source of unity and complexity both in our own minds (in so far as they unite elementary into complex passions) and in our 'world'. 'So far as regards the mind', he writes in the *Abstract* 'these [associations] are the only links that bind the parts of the universe together or connect us with any person or object exterior to ourselves. For as it is by means of thought only that any thing operates upon our passions, and as these are the only ties of our thoughts, they are really *to us* the cement of the universe and all the operations of the mind must, in a great measure, depend upon them' (A, 32). 'So far as regards the mind . . .'; 'to us . . .'—in other words they are the source of all *phenomenal* unity, and hence, so far as Hume writes phenomenalistically, of all unity whatsoever. This is to

[1] *De Memoria et Reminiscentia* (451 B), cf. A. C. Warren, *History of the Associationist Psychology.*

be the most resounding triumph of the science of man. And the science of man itself makes use of associative principles, even at its most purely psychological level, because all but our elementary passions are constructed with their help. That is the main reason why Books I and II of the *Treatise* had to be published as a single work. 'The subjects of the understanding and passions make a compleat chain of reasoning by themselves', so he tells us in the *Advertisement*; and what in particular distinguishes them as a single topic is the fact that in both cases association is the source of order and complexity.

Hume's phrase—'the cement of the universe'—is the metaphor characteristic of atomism; we are to distinguish, within the complexities which confront us, between bricks (elementary perceptions) and cement (associative relations). Association unites our impressions and ideas into the systematic structures which constitute 'reality' for us. The whole project is conceived in Newtonian terms: association is 'a kind of attraction, which in the mental world will be found to have as extraordinary effects as in the natural, and to show itself in as many and as various forms' (T, 13). Previous philosophers had already recognized that association plays a prominent part in the economy of the mind, and 'it is entirely agreeable to the rules of philosophy, and even of common reason; where any principle has been found to have a great force and energy in one instance, to ascribe to it a like energy in all similar instances' (E, 204). As Hartley was to put it (he set out with a Newtonian ambition exactly parallel to Hume's), we begin from certain 'select, well-defined and well-attested phaenomena' and then we proceed 'to explain and predict the other phaenomena by these laws.'[1]

As usual, Locke had unwittingly completed the spade-work. The extent of his contribution to associationist psychology is often underestimated, because it so happens that he introduces the phrase 'association of ideas' (the first occasion of its use) only in the fourth edition of the *Essay*, and then in order to account for such mental aberrations as dreams, not as a theory of orderly thinking. But let us look more closely at what he

[1] *Observations*, Ch. i.

says: 'Some of our ideas have a natural correspondence and connection one with another; it is the office and excellency of our reason to trace these, and hold them together into that union and correspondence which is founded in their peculiar beings. Besides this, there is another connection of ideas wholly owing to chance or custom; ideas that in themselves are not at all of kin, come to be so united in some men's minds that it is very hard to separate them; they always keep in company, and the one no sooner comes into the understanding, but its associate appears with it; and if they are more than two which are thus united, the whole gang, always inseparable, show themselves together.'[1] Locke certainly insists on a distinction between 'necessary' (non-associative) and 'customary' (associative) connexions, but the only 'natural' correspondences with which his theory leaves him are mathematical and moral relationships; in no other case is it possible to show that we unite ideas in accordance with their 'natural correspondence'.

Locke's own argument, then, leads naturally in the direction in which Hume wishes to extend it; once morals have been excluded, the only 'natural correspondences' are the mathematical relationships between ideas. For the rest, every connexion consists in the fact that certain of our ideas customarily go together; the 'connection of ideas wholly owing to chance or custom' is the *typical* case, not an occasional mental aberration.

Hume begins from the case of complexity, the fundamental form of connexion. There is a difficulty in Locke's theory which can be put as follows: if the understanding is a pure capacity for combination, and ideas have no intrinsic connexion one with another, it is impossible to explain why the understanding should conjoin these, rather than those, ideas into complex wholes. Association, Hume believes, is the solution to this problem. Ideas are linked, although not by necessary bonds but by associative 'qualities'; this explains why the same simple ideas 'fall regularly into complex ones' and why different persons regularly form the same complex ideas—as they must

[1] *Essay*, II, xxxiii, 5.

do, since they can successfully communicate by means of language (T, 10).

We are not to ask (again, the appeal is to Newtonian method) *why* association operates as it does; but we can describe *how* it works—by means of resemblance, contiguity, and cause and effect. Just as Newton put aside the search for the causes of attraction, so we must refuse to be led into any discussion of the causes of association. There is, however, a vital difference between the two cases, which Hume fails to recognize. Attraction operates universally: therefore we cannot sensibly ask why it operates in a *particular* case. In contrast, association is only 'a gentle force which commonly prevails'; we are not to conclude that 'without it the mind cannot join two ideas', since 'nothing is more free than that faculty'. Thus there is a genuine problem, and one which Hume does nothing whatever to solve, why association sometimes operates and sometimes fails to operate. Furthermore, sometimes contiguity operates, at other times resemblance; and *one* resembling idea, of the many possible resemblances, exerts the predominant influence—these are facts which Hume leaves unexplained, and which must be explained, if associationism is to be a science of mind. Hobbes had already offered such an explanation: 'the discourse of the mind is nothing but seeking';[1] what we think of next will be associated with what we are now thinking of, but precisely what it is will depend upon the direction of our interests. Hume, on the other hand, leaves us with a 'science of man' which is quite incapable of explaining why our mind works in one way rather than another. This is certainly not Newtonianism; Hume's 'science' is a mere pretence; his associationism can 'explain' *whatever* happens—since it is always possible to say that in this case the 'faculty' exerted its freedom—and this is the surest possible sign that it is not an explanation at all.

Furthermore, there are obvious difficulties in the way of arguing that association can *ever* be the source of complexity. On the face of it, two ideas can resemble one another only if they are already complex, being distinguishable but at the same time having points of resemblance, and can be contiguous as

---

[1] *Leviathan*, Ch. 3.

distinct from coincident only if parts can be discriminated within them. Both these possible objections Hume tries to answer, although in a different context: the first, in a note added in the Appendix to the *Treatise*, the second, in the course of his theory of space and time.

"Tis evident', he argues in the Appendix, 'that even different simple ideas may have a similarity or resemblance to each other; nor is it necessary, that the point or circumstance of resemblance should be distinct or separable from that in which they differ. *Blue* and *green* are different simple ideas, but are more resembling than *blue* and *scarlet*; tho' their perfect simplicity excludes all possibility of separation or distinction. 'Tis the same case with particular sounds, and tastes and smells. These admit of infinite resemblances upon the general appearance and comparison, without having any common circumstance the same. And of this we may be certain, even from the very abstract terms *simple idea*. They comprehend all simple ideas under them. These resemble each other in their simplicity. And yet from their very nature, which excludes all composition, this circumstance, in which they resemble, is not distinguishable nor separable from the rest' (T, 637). This passage was prepared for insertion in his chapter *Of Abstract Ideas*; he there argues that a simple idea can stand for other simple ideas; and the obvious difficulty forces itself upon his attention that unless simple ideas can be different, even although each is nothing but, say, 'blue', the simple and the abstract idea will be quite indistinguishable. But, although it was not designed with this specific intention, his argument, if it could be maintained, would also show how ideas could be simple and yet conjoined by their resemblance into complexities.

Hume's argument is a very curious one: it amounts to saying that simple ideas must at least resemble one another in being simple, so that resemblance is compatible with simplicity. But, of course, if simplicity were genuinely a point of resemblance, the conclusion would rather be that there are no simple ideas: the least which can possibly confront us would be something simple, vivid (or faint) and, for example, blue, i.e. a complex idea. If it never occurs to Hume that this is the natural conclusion of his argument, that it is quite unintelligible to assert that an idea can have various distinguishable characteristics without any sacrifice of its simplicity, this only serves to demonstrate how firmly he is wedded to a particular metaphysics—a belief in ultimate, simple entities.

Suppose, however, we reject the view that simplicity is a point of comparison, suppose we regard 'X is simple' merely as a misleading way of saying that X cannot be characterized except as X, suppose we admit there are ideas of this sort—the question still remains whether they can resemble one another. Hume appeals to examples; but if 'blue and green' are more resembling than 'blue and scarlet', this can only be because they are not simple; they are dull or intense or light or vivid as well as blue or green; or else we see the blue in the green. If all that can be said of blue is that it *is* blue and of green that it *is* green, there is no possible way in which they could resemble one another. This fact comes out very clearly in R. W. Church's attempt at a defence of Hume.[1] 'P_1 and p_2 are similar', he suggests, means precisely the same as 'p_1 is p_1 and p_2 is p_2'. But why do we use 'p' throughout our symbolism? Suppose we were to substitute 'x_1' for 'p_2'. Then it is immediately obvious that 'p_1 and x_1 are similar' is not identical with 'p_1 is p_1 and x_1 is x_1'. The symbolism 'p_1 and p_2' itself *shows* the resemblance, but only by means of its distinction between 'p' (the point of resemblance) and its subscript (the point of difference); Church has quite improperly assumed that simple ideas could replace 'p' in 'p_1 and p_2', which is the very point at issue. And if the distinction is a merely numerical one, assuming this to be possible, it would not serve Hume's purpose: two simple ideas, each qualitatively identical, would not together constitute a new complex idea.

Thus, contiguity (Locke's 'going together') must bear the weight of complexity on its own shoulders. And Hume's theory of space and time is especially designed to combat the view that, as being spatial or temporal, every idea is already complex: the ultimate constituents of our experience, he argues, are indivisible points. That the associationist cannot

[1] *Hume's Theory of the Understanding* (pp. 35-7).

admit infinite divisibility was to be only too clear in the psychology of Hartley. 'Since all sensations', he writes, 'are infinitely divisible, they would not leave any traces or images of themselves, i.e. any ideas . . . unless their infinitesimal parts did cohere together through joint impression i.e. association.'[1] Sensations, he has argued, only *cohere* by association; and yet any sensation we try to select as the unit upon which association can set to work must *already* cohere, in so far as it is further divisible. Hartley tries to make a virtue of his difficulties by an appeal to science; 'one may almost deduce some presumption in favour of the hypothesis here produced, from the mutual indefinite implication of its parts, so agreeable to the tenor of nature in other things'. But, in fact, this 'mutual indefinite implication' is a vicious regress. If every complex sensation has to be constructed out of other sensations, and every sensation is complex, no sensation can ever be constructed. To avoid the regress, one must assert either that complexes are not always constructed or else (in Hume's manner) that there are ultimately simple perceptual units which serve as the starting-point in our constructions.

Yet in thus asserting that extensions are divisible into a finite number of unit parts, Hume is faced with a dilemma: if these parts are themselves extended, one side of them must be distinguishable from the other (i.e. they are divisible); if they are not extended, no number of them could together make up an extension. Hume hopes to avoid this dilemma by ascribing colour or solidity to his spatial points. Thus, he says, he has lit on a medium between the absurdities of 'infinite divisibility' and 'the non-entity of mathematical points' (T, 40). But even supposing that points can be solid or coloured without being divisible in respect of time and place, the problem still remains as it was: how can such points lie alongside one another in such a way as to make up a continuous extension? This is the substantial point of a criticism Hume tries to meet, that 'a simple and indivisible atom, that touches another, must necessarily penetrate it: for 'tis impossible it can touch it by its external parts, from the very supposition of its perfect simplicity,

[1] *Observations*, Prop. XI.

which excludes all parts'. Two points can never lie contiguous to one another, because to be contiguous they would
have to touch only at a certain point; and a point cannot itself
touch at a point except by being that point. Hume cannot
satisfactorily answer this objection. He bids us imagine a red
and a blue point approaching one another. We will 'evidently
perceive', he argues, 'that from the union of these points there
results an object, which is compounded and divisible, and may
be distinguished into two parts, of which each preserves its
existence distinct and separate, notwithstanding its contiguity
to the other' (T, 41). Now, certainly this is something we *can*
imagine, but only because we are not thinking of Hume's
points but rather of patches of colour moving through
continuous space and coming to rest alongside one another. In
a strict sense, Hume is begging the question. An argument has
been brought forward to show that coloured points, understood
as Hume understands them, cannot lie contiguously. Hume,
in reply, asserts that coloured points *can* be contiguous to one
another: but he does not admit the proper conclusion from this
fact—that points cannot be the sort of thing he takes them to be.
He does not, and cannot, directly meet the argument that
contiguity is impossible except between what is already
complex.

In other important respects, as well, Hume's theory of space
and time is important for his associationism. Spatial and
temporal connectedness, it should be observed, is the one form
of union which Hume does not try to derive from association.
This fact has puzzled some of his commentators; Hendel, for
example, argues that 'unless we suppose that imagination
accounts for our actual perception of a world in space and time
through its disposition to unite and connect particular things
in certain ways ultimately peculiar to human nature, we can
hardly understand why this second part of the *Treatise* should
have its important position in the book.'[1] Yet he admits that
Hume makes not the slightest attempt to press this point; and
Hume was not the philosopher to leave his tale unadorned
with the appropriate moral. Nor is it likely, as Hendel suggests,

[1] *Studies in the Philosophy of David Hume*, p. 152.

that Hume's theory of space and time belongs to a very early date, before the possibilities of association had occurred to him. Certainly, and rather surprisingly, Hume had read Bayle, on whom his theory of space and time is heavily dependent, as early as 1732.[1]   But there is no evidence to suggest that associationism was a late accretion to Hume's thinking—its role in the *Treatise* suggests precisely the opposite conclusion.

The fact is that space and time were, in Hume's view, an irreducible minimum of objectivity. 'As to what may be said', he wrote, 'that the operations of nature are independent of our thought and reasoning, I allow it; and accordingly have observ'd, that objects bear to each other the relations of contiguity and succession; that like objects may be observ'd in several instances to have like relations; and that all this is independent of, and antecedent to the operations of the understanding' (T, 168).   Resemblance and contiguity are *there*, in the ideas, from the beginning; *they* cannot be the creation of imagination, because without their aid the imagination, although it could weave fantasies, could never construct a 'world'. Yet, on the other side, if our experience from the beginning is of the form 'here is X', 'there is Y', then propositions, not simple ideas, must be our point of departure. Hume tries to avoid this conclusion by describing space and time (like belief) as a 'manner of appearance', with the suggestion that 'the hereness of X' does not itself appear, but is simply the *manner* of X's appearance. But this doctrine could be made intelligible only—if, indeed, even then—at the cost of a serious departure from the phenomenalist interpretation of ideas *as* appearances. The difficulty, all the while, is that Hume's attempt to restrict objective connexion to resemblance and contiguity puts those relations in a peculiarly privileged position —and he cannot really justify their privilege.

Not only complexity but even the very idea of relation is derived by Hume from associative links. On the face of it, since association is a form of relation, there is at this point a manifest circularity. 'It is evident', writes Laird, 'that perceptions must *be* similar in order to be associated *by* similarity, and that they

[1] E. C. Mossner: *The Life of David Hume*, Nelson, 1954, p. 78.

113

must *have been* contiguous in order to be united by contiguity. For this reason, since resemblance and contiguity are *de facto* relations, it follows that association cannot constitute, but on the contrary presupposes relation.'¹ In reply to this criticism, Hume would certainly insist upon his distinction between two sorts of relation—'natural' and 'philosophical'. It is as a result of the operation of natural relations—the associative connexions which objectively hold between ideas—that we are able to connect ideas together into philosophical relations (i.e. to compare ideas one with another). Hume's distinction between these two sorts of relation is identical with William James's distinction between connexions *thought of*—philosophical relations—and connexions *between thoughts*,² except that Hume would not use the word 'connexion' as a synonym for relation: the relations between our thoughts (associative relations) bring our ideas before our mind in such a way that we can think of these and other relations between them. The relation we think of is sometimes identical with, sometimes quite different from, the relation between our thoughts. Idea A succeeds idea B, perhaps because B resembles A; we might then contemplate this resemblance (as a philosophical relation) or we might, for example, consider some quantitative relation between A and B. The quantitative relation, however, is never the cause of the succession of our ideas: it cannot be a natural relation. Resemblance, contiguity and causality are both natural and philosophical relations: all other relations are merely philosophical. ('When the associations are of successively appearing things', says James, 'the distinction I made at the outset of the chapter between a connexion *thought of* and a connexion *of thoughts* is unimportant. For the connexion thought of is concomitance or succession; and the connexion between the thoughts is just the same.')³ As natural relations, they are what James calls 'mechanical conditions on which thought depends and which determine the order in which is

¹ *Hume's Philosophy*, p. 42.
² *Principles of Psychology*, Vol. 1, p. 551. Here, as elsewhere, James does not seem to be aware that he is merely re-phrasing Hume.
³ *Ibid.*, Vol. 1, p. 565.

presented the content and material for her comparisons';[1] as philosophical relations, they are themselves forms of comparison.

This doctrine, however, even if it may serve to explain in what sense 'relation' can be a product of association, brings awkward problems with it for anyone who abides by the phenomenalist interpretation of 'idea'. How can ideas stand in relations which are not thought of? It is the whole point of ideas that with them, at least, we know where they are; they have no tricks up their sleeves, no unexpected characters to disconcert us, just because they are what they are known as being. But now they threaten to turn into *things*. Association, says Hume, operates 'in so silent and imperceptible a manner that we are scarce sensible of it'; we discover it, he says, 'more by its effects than by any immediate feeling or perception' (T, 305). But this, of course, is quite inconsistent with Hume's theory of causality; unless association is constantly conjoined with its effects *in our experience*, it makes no sense to say that these are 'its effects'. The fact is, once more, that without assuming an initial 'cement' Hume cannot move a step; he has to begin from a 'universe' in which things are *actually* contiguous and *actually* have certain effects, being united in relations which are none of our work. The most he can say is that certain kinds of union are the product of other kinds of union; without original unions, union cannot be constructed.

We can now state Hume's position more precisely, making use of a contrast which he often, although not in an absolutely consistent way, himself employs—the contrast between 'connexion' and 'conjunction'. Hume will quite happily remark that 'the mind never perceives any real connexion among distinct existences' (T, 636), even although he has steadily affirmed that our perceptions, for all their distinctness, are 'connected together in the imagination' (T, 13) by associative relations. This connexion by the imagination is a conjunction, not a 'real connexion', just because it does not compromise the distinctness of our perceptions. That there are *objective* conjunctions and repetitions Hume takes for granted

[1] *Principles of Psychology*, Vol. i, p. 553.

(however difficult it may be for him to account for them); and he admits also (which is a still greater difficulty) that these conjunctions and repetitions have certain *objective* effects upon our mind. But 'the universe' which, he thought, we envisage in common life and try to describe in science does not consist of conjoined perceptions; it is made up of complex substances, persistent through a series of changes, which operate upon other similar substances. Qualities inhere in substances, substances have distinguishable phases, and are necessarily connected one with another; these are forms of connexion, as distinct from conjunction, because in asserting them we deny the 'distinctness' (the self-sufficiency) of our perceptions. The problem is to show how mere conjunction (together with that simple connexion—'only a little one'—between conjunctions and our imagination) can engender our belief in such a 'Universe'.

Causal connexion, on Hume's analysis of it, fitted very neatly into this pattern: a fact which must have given heart to his whole associationist project, and which enabled him in the *Abstract* (where causality is picked out as the main theme of the *Treatise*) still to congratulate himself on its success. As a relation which holds between perceptions it can be reduced to the repetition of similar conjunctions (T, 170; E, 77); as a connexion it consists merely in the fact that, under the influence of these conjunctions, the mind passes readily from one perception to another. That most important form of 'cementing', then— causal connexion—would form no part of the Universe *for us* (at least), were it not for the influence of association. But even in this case, association is not quite sufficient; Hume, as we saw, has to introduce an 'irregular' propensity in order to account for the way in which we project necessity from our own mind into the perceptions which we take to be necessarily connected. The role of this propensity is a relatively slight one; but the need for it is a warning of things to come. For the other major forms of connexion, those considered in Part IV of the *Treatise*, invoke irregular propensities to a degree which admitted of no disguise or exculpation.

The case of independent and continuous existence is worth

considering at some length. Our 'senses' (which now include memory) do not directly acquaint us with *continuous* existence—it would be, Hume says, a 'contradiction in terms' to suppose that the senses perceived that their objects continued to exist after the senses ceased to perceive them (T, 188). Nor could they suggest to us the idea of *distinct* existence. ('Distinct existence', at this point, means existence *independent of our perceptions*; this must not be confused with the 'distinct existence' of our 'distinct perceptions'.) The senses convey to us a single perception, not that perception and something else beyond it; so if by 'distinct existence' we mean the existence of something else *as well as* our perception in the manner of theories of representative perception, this 'something else' must be an inference. Our impressions do not confront us *as* copies. Nor are we aware of the perception itself ('by a kind of fallacy and illusion') as something which exists independently of us. If we know a perception as 'a thing perceived by us', we must be constantly perceiving ourselves, which is far from being the case, as is shown by the difficulty we have in giving any account of our nature. In any case, 'every impression, external and internal [is] originally on the same footing'; each appears in its 'true colours', each is known as an impression or idea. Our senses can no more deceive us about their 'relations and situation' than about their characters. 'For since all actions and sensations of the mind are known to us by consciousness, they must necessarily appear in every particular what they are, and be what they appear' (T, 190). To think otherwise, 'were to suppose, that even where we are most intimately conscious, we might be mistaken'; and this, to Hume, is a genuine *reductio ad absurdum*. If, then, we were to rely upon the evidence of our senses, our 'Universe' would consist of discontinuous perceptions.

Reason, equally, cannot be the source of our ordinary belief in distinct and continuous existence; for this belief is strong in men who know nothing of the arguments by which philosophers have tried to establish that there are external objects. Ordinary men, indeed, persist in the belief that 'the very things they feel or see' are possessed of a distinct and continuous existence, a belief which Reason, far from originating, can show to be irrational; for 'philosophy informs us, that every thing, which appears to the mind, is nothing but a perception, and is interrupted, and dependent on the mind' (T, 193).

The decks have now been cleared for action. Our belief in distinct and continuous existence originates neither in Reason nor Sense; imagination must therefore be its sponsor. The question now is what qualities in our perceptions provoke the imagination to 'give rise to so extraordinary an opinion' (T, 195). These qualities will play the same role in relation to our belief in distinct and continuous existence as did constant conjunction in relation to our belief in necessary connexion. The 'vulgar opinion' that the involuntariness of certain perceptions—'their superior force and violence'—points to their independence and continuity will not suffice, since pains may also be involuntary, forceful and violent, and yet no one concludes that they must therefore be external and continuous. The crucial qualities are *constancy* ('my bed and table, my books and papers, present themselves in the same uniform manner, and change not upon account of any interruption in my seeing or perceiving them' (T, 194)), and *coherence* ('When I return to my chamber after an hour's absence, I find not my fire in the same situation,. in which I left it: but then I am accustom'd in other instances to see a like alteration produc'd in a like time, whether I am present or absent, near or remote' (T, 195)). Hume's problem can now be expressed as follows: can these qualities be reduced to the regular associative links? If 'constancy' is simply a form of resemblance, and 'coherence' is causality, and if between them these can account for our belief in external and independent existence, then associationism has proved itself once more.

Hume begins with coherence. He supposes himself to be seated at a desk, to hear a distinctive sound 'as of a door turning upon its hinges', and then to see a porter coming towards him. 'This gives rise to many new reflexions and reasonings. First, I never have observ'd that this noise cou'd proceed from anything but the motion of a door; and therefore conclude, that the present phenomenon is a contradiction to all past experience unless the door, which I remember on t'other side the chamber, be still in being.' So far it looks as if the reduction of coherence to causality can be successfully accomplished; for the argument from sound to door is just the familiar reasoning from effects to causes. But he goes further: 'I have always found, that a human being was possess't of a quality, which I call gravity, and which hinders it from mounting into the air, as this porter must have done to arrive at my chamber, unless the stairs I remember be not annihilated by my absence.' And further still: 'I receive a letter, which upon opening it I perceive by the hand-writing to have come from a friend, who says he is two hundred leagues distant. 'Tis evident, I can never account for this phenomenon, conformable to my experience in other instances, without spreading out in my mind the whole sea and continent between us, and supposing the effects and continu'd existence of posts and ferries, according to my memory and observation' (T, 196).

From a small group of objects, then, 'contained in a few yards around me', I create a world. Now, creation on this scale, as Hume sees, lies beyond the powers of habit. Habit might lead us to have a vivid idea of a door (to regard it, that is, as a 'real existence'), but it could never lead us beyond the door, to a world which is not *constantly* conjoined with our present experience. ''Tis evident, that whenever we infer the continu'd existence of the objects of sense from their coherence, and the frequency of their union, 'tis in order to bestow on the objects a greater regularity than what is observ'd in our mere perceptions' (T, 197). Even in the case of objects which actually confront us, 'the turning about of our head, or the shutting of our eyes' is able to destroy the regularity of our experience. And, of course, we have not even a *single* experience of the chain of events which leads from the posting of a letter in a foreign country to our receipt of it.

Unfortunately, Hume does not make this point with sufficient clarity; in consequence, his commentators have some-times accused him of forgetting that, in Laird's words, 'his doctrine of causality was a doctrine of association *beyond* actua: experience'.[1] But, in fact, Hume is now realizing just what a

[1] *Hume's Philosophy*, p. 149.

short distance this 'beyond' can carry him: it cannot lead even to a belief in conjunctions which have a greater regularity than the conjunctions we have actually perceived, still less to a belief in the existence of causal sequences which lie quite beyond the range of our actual experience.

Thus, Hume suggests, another 'principle'—another 'irregular propensity'—has to be invoked. 'The imagination, when set into any train of thinking, is apt to continue, even when its object fails it' (T, 198). He insists, once again, that he has pointed to this propensity on a previous occasion, and therefore cannot be charged with setting up *ad hoc* hypotheses. That there is such a 'propensity' we can, I should say, admit— we often suppose that regularities exist even when our experience shows no such regularity (although on other occasions we *deny* regularities in the face of all the evidence). But these supposals, and these denials, rest upon our experience of continuities, and of the advantages and disadvantages we derive from them. They cannot, therefore, *account for* that experience. Perhaps that is why Hume considers this propensity 'too weak to support alone so vast an edifice, as is that of the continu'd existence of all external bodies' (T, 198); but, in any case, to grant to it so extensive a potency would be to abandon associationism, and that Hume has no intention of doing. Coherence, Hume has now admitted, cannot be reduced to causality; but there is still constancy to be taken into account. Perhaps the regular associative relations will in this case be more successful.

The first problem is to show how the mere resemblance between our perceptions could lead us to a belief in continuous and distinct existence. In a manner characteristic of this part of the *Treatise*, Hume argues that the close resemblance between our perceptions induces us to ascribe to them an actual identity. But that resemblance *of itself*, he admits, would not be sufficient. The mind experiences 'a smooth and uninterrupt'd progress' in passing from a perception to a closely resembling perception: this feeling of ease is very like the feeling we experience when we are considering a genuinely unchanging object. 'The thought slides along the succession with equal facility, as if it consider'd only one object; and therefore confounds the succession with the identity' (T, 204). How this confusion could occur Hume cannot possibly explain, seeing that 'all actions of the mind . . . must necessarily appear in every particular what they are, and be what they appear' (T, 190). But apart from that, and even at this preliminary stage in Hume's argument, association has again proved inadequate for its task —it has to be supplemented by 'thought' which 'considers' our perceptions and confuses one with another.

The next problem is to account for the fact that the actual experienced interruptedness of our perceptions does not destroy our tendency to ascribe identity to them: we unite our perceptions, he suggests, 'by the fiction of a continued existence' in order to reconcile the facility with which we pass from one perception to another with their actual interruptedness. Thus yet another 'propensity' is invoked; the mind when confronted by contradictions feels 'a sensible uneasiness'; it creates fictions in order to overcome this uneasiness. The mechanical links between our ideas could not *of themselves* generate fictions: the co-operation of 'our mind' is vital, as we have already seen, and as Hume here substantially admits.

And how, even then, can we assent to 'so palpable a contradiction' as that a perception may exist without actually being present to the mind? (Hume is now discussing the 'vulgar' view, which, on his interpretation, identifies perceptions and objects —so that, for it, an 'unperceived object' would be an 'unperceived perception'.) This possibility can be 'feigned', Hume suggests—in other words it does not involve a manifest contradiction—because we can conceive a perception as breaking off from that collection of perceptions which constitutes a mind. He has still to explain the origin of our belief that this is what *in fact* happens. By what means, in other words, is vivacity transferred to the idea of continued existence? (It has no vivacity of its own, not being an 'impression of the senses or memory'.) Its vividness ought to be derived, on Hume's general theory, from a related impression, by means of associative links. But Hume now suggests that such associative transfers of vivacity are never mechanical; they must always make use of the mediation of 'the mind'. 'The mind falls so easily from the one perception to the other . . . that it scarce perceives the change, but retains in the second a considerable share of the vivacity of the first. It is excited by the lively impression; and this vivacity is convey'd to the related idea, without any great diminution in the passage, by reason of the smooth transition and the propensity of the imagination' (T, 208). Then if this same 'propensity' arises from some *other* principle—'besides that of relation'— it can operate in the same vivifying way. That is what happens in the present case. We have a vast number of 'impressions of the memory' (which are by this time quite as good as impressions proper); these excite in us a propensity to feign 'the continued existence of all sensible objects'; and this feigning is converted into a belief, as the result of the effect in our mind of the vivacity of the impressions. We go so far as to ascribe a continuous existence 'to objects which are perfectly new to us and of whose constancy and coherence we have no experience'; in such cases 'the manner, in which they present themselves to our senses, resembles that of constant and coherent objects' (T, 209).

It would be pointless to comment in detail on the twists and turns of this devious argument. But the tangle is characteristic. Association is not entirely neglected; resemblance, especially, plays an important part in Hume's argument. It is supplemented, however, by a multitude of 'propensities' (the very thing which a consistent associationism would hope to avoid), and without their aid—without the continual intervention of 'mind' as distinct from mechanical relations between perceptions—Hume's argument would be totally ineffective. Indeed, associationism comes to be a special example, only, of a much more general principle, the principle that the mind moves in whatever direction will bring it most ease. After all that Hume has had to say about the origins of belief, we find him insisting that 'a strong propensity or inclination alone, without any present impression, will sometimes cause a belief or opinion' (T, 210). The mind's own interests and inclinations rather than the conjunctions and repetitions of its perceptions come to be 'the cement of the Universe'. Certain of our perceptions, he has argued, are in no respect spatial—they have neither extension nor position and yet we ordinarily speak of them as existing in certain particular places. We ascribe a certain taste (the taste of a fig, for example) to a particular extended body, even although a non-extended perception like a taste cannot possibly be spatially conjoined with an extended body (T, 236). How is this illusion generated? In the first place, the fig's taste and smell are *temporally* inseparable from its colour and tangibility, and this unites them into a causal sequence. 'Whichever of them be the cause or effect, 'tis certain they are always co-existent.' Not even priority in time, apparently, is now necessary to causal connexion. And then, also, they are 'co-temporary in the time of their appearance to the mind', since ''tis upon the application of the extended body to our senses we perceive its particular taste and smell'. By thus ingeniously passing backwards and forwards between objects and perceptions, Hume manages to extract two associative relations from a single fact—the fact that colour and taste occur at the same time. But even these two relations ('causation and contiguity in the time of their appearance') will not together suffice to generate our 'illusion'. The transition from colour and tangibility to taste is not sufficiently 'easy and natural' to suit our exigent minds. Yet another propensity emerges from its hiding-place: 'when objects are united by any relation, we have a strong propensity to add some new relation to them, in order to compleat the union' (T, 237). This propensity, he again insists, has not been invented for this occasion—we have already seen it at work (T, 217); but the present case is the real 'evidence' that it exists. The fact is that Hume can now draw upon an unsystematized list of propensities, gradually accumulated in the course of the *Treatise*; without their aid the associative 'cement' would immediately crumble into sand.

Difficulties of a parallel kind beset Hume's associationist theory of the passions; in this case, however, he never pretends to be a fully-fledged associationist: he does not think that *all* the passions consist in the association of certain perceptions with pleasure or with pain. Such a theory had been adumbrated by Hobbes, and it was worked out in some detail by John Gay in his *Concerning the Fundamental Principles of Virtue and Morality* (1731). Gay's essay was published as a 'preliminary dissertation' to an English translation of a very well-known work, William King's *De Origine Mali*, to which Hume refers in his *Dialogues* (D, 194). It is not unlikely that Hume had Gay (among others) in mind when, in the *Principles of Morals*, he attacks 'Hobbists and Epicureans' (E, 296). In any case, his criticism is certainly directed against associationist Utilitarianism, which arises, in Hume's somewhat self-righteous words, from 'that love of *simplicity* which has been the source of much false reasoning in philosophy' (E, 298). 'To the most careless observer', he writes, 'there appears to be such dispositions as benevolence and generosity; such affections as love, friendship, compassion, gratitude. These sentiments have their causes, effects, objects and operations, marked by common language and observation, and plainly distinguished from those of the selfish passions.' In the *Treatise* he expresses the matter thus: certain of our passions arise 'directly' in our mind, whether from pain or pleasure or 'from a natural impulse or instinct, which is perfectly unaccountable' (T, 439). With these 'direct' passions Hume does not much concern himself (just as he is not very much interested in impressions and ideas, as such); the central psychological problem is to construct the more complicated 'indirect passions' out of the direct passions, with the aid of the associative principles.

The passions he considers in most detail are pride and 'its direct contrary'—humility (T, 277). These passions have the same *object*; when we are actuated by either of them 'the view always fixes' upon ourselves. The self, however, cannot be the *cause* of these passions; the cause cannot be something common to pride and humility since we could not then explain why sometimes one passion arises and sometimes the other. On the face of it, each has a multitude of causes—'every valuable quality' of the mind, of the body, or of anything 'in the least ally'd or related to us' can be a source of pride, and its opposite, of humility (T, 279). But Hume thinks that he can greatly simplify this apparent heterogeneity of causes. First, he distinguishes between the *quality* which arouses pride and the *subject* (i.e. 'substance') in which the quality appears. The beauty of our house is the quality in it which arouses our pride; but beauty itself does not arouse pride, if it is not ours, nor are we proud of everything that is ours. Looking in this way at the causes of pride, we see, Hume argues, that the quality which assists in the production of pride is always one which *gives us pleasure*, and the subject in which that quality inheres *always bears some relation to ourselves* (T, 285). Considering now the passion of pride itself, Hume undertakes a parallel analysis: pride is a *pleasant* sensation—he goes so far as to say that pleasure constitutes its 'very being and essence' (T, 286)—and it is always *directed towards ourselves*. Thus there is an association of impressions (this has now been officially added to the association of ideas, although a 'remarkable difference' has been insisted upon—it operates 'only by resemblance' (T, 283)) between the sensation of pleasure which the quality of the subject produces in us and the pleasant sensation of pride itself; and, along with this, an association of ideas between the idea of ourselves and the idea of what belongs to us. This double association gives rise to an easy transition from the presence of a pleasant property in something we own to the passion of pride. And we can readily understand why pride so rapidly turns into humility; for humility is identical with pride in its object (ourselves) and in the character of the subject which causes it (something belonging to us). As soon, then, as the *quality* of that subject changes (e.g. our house becomes dilapidated) our pride is rapidly converted into humility.

This analysis has the same importance in Hume's theory of the passions as causality has in his theory of the understanding; in this case, and in this case only, the associative mechanism needs relatively slight assistance from additional propensities. Even so, Hume—shall we say 'with endearing candour' or with 'an exasperating disregard for consistency'?—admits 'certain limitations to this system'. Not every pleasant object which is related to ourselves makes us proud; the relation must be 'a close one'; the object must be substantially 'peculiar to ourselves', 'obvious to others' and 'durable' (T, 291-2). 'General rules', too, enter once more into the picture—a person may be proud of an object from which he does not derive, thanks to some peculiarity of health or temperament, the slightest pleasure, if there is a 'general rule' that such objects are a sign of rank. Hume had hoped to initiate a Copernican revolution in the theory of passions. Moral philosophy, he said, 'is in the same condition as natural, with regard to astronomy before the time of Copernicus'; it was his task to replace its 'intricate systems' with something more 'easy and natural'; he spoke with scorn of those who 'invent without scruple a new principle to every new phenomenon, instead of adapting it to the old' (T, 282). But complications would rear their ugly head.

There are other difficulties, aside from these 'limitations', in Hume's theory of pride and humility. He is certainly not entitled, for example, to talk of an 'idea of ourselves'—which becomes, when he needs an extra supply of vivacity, 'the idea or rather impression of ourselves' (T, 317);[1] and his transitions between independent things, which alone can be 'closely related to us' and 'obvious to others', and ideas, which alone can be associated, are even more blatant than those he regularly allows himself. A particularly important problem arises out of his description of the passions—which, after all, are only 'impressions'—as having 'objects'. The fact is that Hume never really thinks out the relation between his epistemology and his theory of passions; sometimes 'the view' (whatever this is) 'fixes on ourselves', when pride 'actuates us' (T, 277); sometimes pride 'produces' the idea of the self (T, 287); sometimes pride is described as something which can never 'look beyond self' (T, 286). If what really happens is that pride 'produces' the idea of self, that idea will be its effect, not its object; if, on the other hand, pride *itself* views the self, this will involve a complete revision of Hume's epistemology. The consequences will be no less far-reaching if pride somehow provokes the mind to have an idea of itself; and in this case, too, that idea is

[1] Hume is echoing Malebranche: 'Nous n'avons point d'idée claire d'aucune modification de notre âme. Il n'y a que le sentiment intérieur qui nous apprenne que nous sommes, et ce que nous sommes' (Ier Eclaircissement to *Recherche*, Vol. IV, p. 20, 1762 edition).

in no sense the 'object' of pride, but only an idea which regularly occurs *later than* pride.

These difficulties are accentuated in Hume's theory of love and hate, for whereas pride and humility can with some plausibility be represented as 'pure emotions in the soul' (passive *consequences*), love and hate, as Hume recognizes, 'are not compleated within themselves, nor rest in that emotion which they produce, but carry the mind to something farther' (T, 367). And in the course of his examination of these passions, Hume comes, as he puts it, 'to be sensible, in some measure, of a misfortune, that has attended every system of philosophy, with which the world has been yet acquainted' (T, 366)— a misfortune, none the less, which he had expected the science of mind entirely to avoid. He is confronted by phenomena for which his system cannot account. These phenomena, so he hastens to reassure us, do not actually *contradict* his system; they do, however, involve some departure from 'that simplicity which hath been hitherto its principal force and beauty'. He had hoped to show that there is a precise parallel between love and pride, between hate and humility ; but the 'incompleteness'—the dynamic character—of love and hate destroys the parallelism. The day can only be saved by supposing that love is 'conjoined with' benevolence and hatred with anger; thus love, through this conjunction, seeks the happiness of its object, and anger its misery. This conjunction is of a peculiarly intimate kind, to which ideas present no parallel. 'Ideas never admit of a total union, but are endow'd with a kind of impenetrability. . . . On the other hand, impressions and passions are susceptible of an entire union; and, like colours, may be blended so perfectly together, that each of them may lose itself' (T, 366). Thus Hume embarks upon a 'mental chemistry' —'the passions', he says in the *Dissertation*, 'are like an alkali and an acid, which being mingled, destroy each other'.[1] This is a far cry from 'distinct existences' linked only by associative relations.

There is no need to follow Hume through the multiplication of his concessions. Passions gradually become less and less like

[1] G.G., IV, 143.

sensations. We find him, for example, contrasting 'the faculty of the passions' with 'the faculty of the imagination' (T, 339) and describing the passions as 'a more powerful principle than the imagination' (T, 344), even though, if they are to be subject to the laws of association, the passions must stand to the imagination as raw material to an artificer. Resemblance, Hume has said, is the sole form of association between passions; but new forms gradually emerge—'the parallel direction of the desires is a real relation, and no less than a resemblance in their sensation, produces a connexion among them . . . any principal desire may be attended with subordinate ones, which are connected with it, and to which if other desires are parallel, they are by that means related to the principal one' (T, 394). In short, a species of sentimentalism gradually replaces Hume's associationism.

How far was he conscious of the deficiencies in his association-ism? Clearly, he did not wish entirely to abandon it. In that condensed and desultory work, *A Dissertation on the Passions*, he still insists that 'the present theory of the passions depends entirely upon the double relations of sentiments and ideas, and the mutual assistance, which these relations lend to each other';[1] and he concludes with the warning that he has by no means exhausted his subject, that 'it is sufficient for my purpose, if I have made it appear, that, in the production and conduct of the passions, there is a certain regular mechanism which is susceptible of as accurate a disquisition as the laws of motion, optics, hydrostatics, or any part of natural philosophy'.[2]

If we had no other evidence, we should certainly suppose that the *Dissertation* is so unsatisfactory only because it is a sketch-plan; Hume could well have discovered, when he came to write it, that his intricate arguments could not be successfully abbreviated—and might have intended the *Dissertation* only as a way of drawing attention to the *Treatise*. But these unabated claims for association contrast oddly with the changes which have come over his theory of sympathy. In the *Treatise* this is one of the most important applications of the associationist psychology. First invoked in order to explain our 'love of fame'

[1] *Ed. cit.*, p. 158.   [2] *Ed. cit.*, p. 166.

or 'concern for the opinion of others', it turns out to be the most potent of our propensities (T, 316); by means of it, we 'receive by communication' from other people 'their inclinations and sentiments, however different from, and even contrary to our own'. Causal inference from 'external signs' supplies us with our evidence that other people have affections: but it provides us with no more than an *idea* of these affections (one must simply forget Hume's general theory of causality). 'Sympathy' involves the conversion of this idea into an impression which 'acquires such a degree of force and vivacity, as to become the very passion itself' (T, 317); this conversion is the work of other associative relations. The passion with which we sympathize *resembles* our passions; we sympathize only with those who are physically close to us (contiguity), or are related to us by blood ('a species of causation'), or are acquaintances of ours (acquaintance 'operates in the same manner with education and custom') (T, 318). All these co-operating influences succeed in turning our idea into an impression.

This argument involves the abandoning of every distinction between impressions and ideas except liveliness; but, even then, our 'idea' is of 'X's being angry', not simply of 'anger'—we sympathize with a particular *person*—and however vivid this becomes it can never be converted into *my* anger; for such a conversion would involve a change in content, as well as in vividness. For this or other reasons, a quite different theory of sympathy is developed in *The Principles of Morals*. Newton is played against Newton; 'we must stop somewhere in our examination of causes'; why not stop at sympathy? 'It is not probable' that sympathy can be 'resolved into principles more simple and universal, whatever attempts have been made to that purpose' (E, 219n). So far at least, and at a very important point, the associationist analysis of passions has been modified. But, after all, Hume had always emphasized that there are 'natural' passions, which cannot be associatively analysed, but must be taken as given: to add one more to his list was not to abandon associationism.

What of his associationist theory of the understanding? In the *Treatise* he has confessed that association is not enough:

'the understanding, when it acts alone, and according to its most general principles, entirely subverts itself' (T, 267). Were it not for 'the trivial suggestions of the fancy' (i.e. its non-associative propensities) we should collapse into total scepticism. And yet it is in the *Abstract* that he makes his most sweeping claims for association; and these claims, as we saw, are unmitigated in the *Dissertation*. The first *Enquiry*, however, is much more circumspect; association is no longer compared to gravitation. The fact remains that, in all but the last edition, there is a long passage in which Hume extends association into yet another field—that of aesthetics. He was still intent, so much is obvious, on employing associationist principles over the whole range of the moral sciences. He adds a note to the effect that 'these loose hints [may] beget a suspicion at least, if not a full persuasion, that this subject is very copious, and that many operations of the human mind depend upon the connexion or association of ideas which is here explained'; and he concludes thus: 'the full explication of this principle and all its consequences would lead us into reasonings too profound and too copious for this enquiry.'[1] It is, then, partly as an effect of his new literary policy—to avoid reasonings which are 'too profound and too copious'—that he places so little stress on association in the *Enquiry*. In the fourth edition, however, this passage disappears; perhaps Hume, towards the end of his career, was finally weaned from his associationist ambitions.

But why was the process so gradual, for all that he makes concession after concession? For one thing, he was determined to develop a science of man; no *systematic* psychology except associationism lay ready to his hand—his sentimentalist psychology (for all that he had Hutcheson and Shaftesbury to draw upon) was a thing of shreds and patches. Nor did any other psychology promise so well, whether as an ingredient in his psychological positivism or as contribution to his critique of formal logic. (It is no accident that 'empirical logic' has so often been combined with an associationist psychology.) The most Hume could do, without seriously disrupting more than one of his major intentions, was to restrict the range of

[1] G.G., IV, 19-23n. This passage is not printed in Selby-Bigge.

his associationism, 'supplementing' it at one point after another; to abandon it entirely would have been ruinous to the whole scheme of his philosophy. And the supplementations had to be modestly, almost surreptitiously, introduced, if Hume was still to represent himself as a great simplifier, in the style of Newton and Copernicus.

Hume, it must again be emphasized, had a quite extraordinary insensitivity to consistency; few men are so ready to announce a general principle and admit exceptions to it, all in a single breath, or, having admitted exceptions, still to proceed as if they did not exist. Perhaps, too, Hume was sentimentally attached to 'association'. In his letter to Dr. George Cheyne he tells us that 'about the age of 18 years of age' there seemed to be opened up to him 'a new scene of Thought'.[1] It is not possible quite definitely to determine in what this 'new scene of thought' consisted—Kemp Smith[2] suggests that it was the discovery that science, no less than morals, rested on 'feeling'. But when we consider the way in which Hume clung, at all costs, to the theory of association, the way in which, in the *Abstract*, he insists upon that theory, above all others, as the novelty which he has introduced into philosophy, the way in which he returns to it again and again, as the cord which will lead him safely through the labyrinth of philosophy, we may more than suspect that associationism was the 'new scene of thought', the foundation of his 'philosophical enquiries' into the moral sciences. And then it is easier than ever to understand his devoted attachment to association, the first great idea of his youth. And it was on association, after all, that Hume rested his claim to be the Newton of the moral sciences, the ambition, surely, which was most likely, in the intellectual atmosphere of the time, to inflame his youthful enthusiasm.

[1] *Letters*, Vol. 1, p. 23. Mossner suggests that this letter was to Dr. John Aburthnot. See E. C. Mossner: *Life of David Hume* (p. 84). Mossner's researches have also made it clear that, when he wrote this letter, Hume had read King's *De Origine Mali*, in the edition which includes John Gay's preliminary essay. This means that he was acquainted from an early age with a worked-out associationist position. (See Mossner's *Life*, p. 80 and my p. 124 above.)

[2] *David Hume*, p. 20.

CHAPTER VII

THE SCEPTIC

HUME takes scepticism very seriously; in this respect, as in so many others, his attitude is that of a French rather than a British philosopher. In France, scepticism was a live issue; but immense volumes like de Crousaz' *Examen du Pyrrhonisme Ancien et Moderne* (1733) had no British analogue. When Berkeley inveighed against 'the sceptics', the scepticism he had in mind was a relatively milk-and-water affair, very different from the hardy speculations of Montaigne and Bayle. It had two principal constituents: the doctrine that we cannot 'penetrate into the inward essence and constitution of things', and the doctrine that 'the mind of man being finite' it is bound to run into 'absurdities and contradictions' when it 'treats of things which partake of Infinity'.[1] Hume quite liked scepticism in this, the Locke-Malebranche form; he made use of it in his assault on metaphysics and in chastening the pretensions of physical science. Pyrrhonism was a different matter: a useful servant, in so far as it was directed against the possibility of solving philosophical doubts by philosophical methods, it threatened to become the master, and to destroy the science of man itself.

And yet Hume's imagination certainly responded to the daring and sweep of Pyrrhonism, as Bayle described it. 'An attempt to run down all science', Bayle wrote, 'and to reject not only the testimony of Sense, but that of Reason too, is the boldest that ever was formed in the Republic of Letters. It is like that of the Alexanders, and other conquerors who would subdue all nations.'[2]

Bold projects of this sort appealed to Hume; his object, according to the Introduction to the *Treatise*, is 'to march up directly to the capital or centre of these sciences, to human

---

[1] *Principles*, Introduction § 2. The Newtonian view we have already met (p. 50); the Arnauld-Malebranche doctrine we shall discuss later.

[2] *Dictionary*, art. *Arcesilas*, Note G.

nature itself; which being once masters of, we may every where else hope for an easy victory' (T, xx). Still, it was science he hoped to conquer; and Pyrrhonism threatened to turn his dominions into a dream-kingdom. The sceptical project which Bayle envisaged was one Hume could quite easily compass; and yet, at the same time, he had no intention of permanently persisting in a sceptical conclusion. Science, not merely peace of mind, was his objective; this fact sharply separated him from the classical sceptics.

In the *Treatise*, the scepticism which Hume learnt from Bayle simply overlays the positivist-associationist structure of his original argument; in consequence, Hume lapses into inconsistencies of the most startling character. Knowledge and probability are sharply distinguished from one another —and yet 'all knowledge resolves itself into probability' (T, 181); the trivial operations of the fancy are 'neither unavoidable to mankind, nor necessary . . . but, on the contrary, are observed only to take place in weak minds' (T, 225)—and yet 'a resolution to reject all the trivial suggestions of the fancy . . . wou'd be dangerous, and attended with the most fatal consequences' (T, 267). The bewilderment Hume displays at the end of Book I of the *Treatise* is genuine enough, although, unable to resist the opportunity scepticism offers him for self-dramatization, he lapses into a stagey, melodramatic tone. ('I cannot forebear feeding my despair, with all those desponding reflections, which the present subject furnishes me with in such abundance' (T, 264).) By the time he came to write the *Enquiries* and the *Dialogues on Natural Religion*, his feelings, his ideas, and his 'literary' impulses were under better control; we shall understand his sceptical intentions more clearly if we make these later writings our point of departure, referring back, as the need arises, to the more detailed arguments of the *Treatise*.

In the *Enquiry*, Hume begins (E, 149) by asking what is meant by 'scepticism': a very necessary question, since although 'divines and graver philosophers' are constantly provoked to indignation by this 'enemy of religion' no one has ever met the creature they triumphantly refute—'who had no opinion or principle concerning any subject, either of action or speculation'.

In this sense of the word, there are no sceptics. What, then, is the real identity of 'the sceptic'? 'How far is it possible to push these philosophical principles of doubt and uncertainty?'

First of all, there is *antecedent* scepticism, of the sort recommended by the Cartesians; they advise us to doubt even our own faculties. It is *possible*, they argue, that our faculties deceive us, and until that possibility can be removed we ought not to trust them. They ask for some guarantee that our faculties are reliable, a guarantee resting upon a self-evident first principle. But, Hume argues, there is no such first principle, nor, if there were, could we advance a step beyond it 'but by the use of those very faculties, of which we are supposed to be already diffident'. The Cartesian doubt, therefore, if we could take it seriously (as we plainly cannot do), 'would be entirely incurable' (E, 150).

This antecedent scepticism is closely related to the 'scepticism with regard to reason' which Hume presents in the *Treatise*, although it is there commingled, as it is in Descartes, with what Hume calls 'consequent scepticism'—the scepticism which arises out of our discovery that our faculties not only might, but do in fact, lead us into error. Hume's argument runs roughly as follows: we know that we sometimes make mistakes, even in mathematics, and therefore we cannot rely uncritically on our Reason. Suppose we ascribe to it a degree of reliability R. But now we reflect that it is only by relying upon our Reason that we have come to ascribe this degree of reliability to it. Hence, the proposition 'our Reason has the degree of reliability R' has only the reliability R; but that it has this degree of reliability we discover only with the help of our Reason and so this new assertion has only the reliability R . . . a regress *ad infinitum*. 'Let our first belief be never so strong, it must infallibly perish by passing thro' so many new examinations, of which each diminishes somewhat of its force and vigour.' Thus we are reduced to an utter scepticism: 'all the rules of logic require a continual diminution, and at last a total extinction of belief and evidence' (T, 183).

This argument has been severely criticized; Reid examines it at length,[1] and Prichard follows closely in Reid's footsteps.[2]

[1] *Essay*, VII, § 4.   [2] *Knowledge and Perception*, pp. 192-6.

In judging a proposition to have a certain reliability, they object, we are saying that it has *in fact* this degree of reliability; the general reflection that our Reason is fallible (that we *sometimes* make mistakes) can do nothing to disturb our conviction that in this particular case we have not made a mistake. If it is certain that two and two make four, then this *is* certain, however fallible our faculties may be.

But Hume, it must be remembered, is working within the Cartesian tradition; and within that tradition his argument is effective *ad hominem*. The Cartesian assumption was that '*p*' is certain only if '*p*' is known by an infallible method; similarly, Hume suggests, '"*p*" is probable' must mean that '"*p*" is known by faculties which are *usually* reliable'. With this assumption made explicit, Hume's argument runs thus: no faculty is infallible, hence '*p*' is never certain; the probability of '*p*' will be proportionate to the reliability of the faculties which discover it; we shall need an investigation to determine the reliability of those faculties; the results of this new investigation are reliable only in proportion to the reliability of the faculties which undertake *that* investigation. . . . The Cartesians had avoided such a regress either by finding in God an ultimate guarantee of reliability, or else (in order to avoid the 'Cartesian circle') by assuming that the reliability of our faculties could be, as it were, 'read off' by those faculties themselves. Thus Locke exhorts us to 'survey our understandings' in order to find out what we can know; it never occurs to him there could be any difficulty in undertaking this survey itself or that it might just as much need a guarantee as any other investigation. Propositions about our faculties, in this tradition, are in a peculiarly privileged position: their reliability, alone, remains unquestioned. What Hume is suggesting is that they have no claim to any such privilege; if that is so, this neo-Cartesian analysis of probability leads inevitably to a regress.

The regress is a vicious one: this analysis demands that we stop at a certain point (the examination of our faculties) in the estimation of reliabilities, and yet it can provide no explanation why, if we must proceed to that point, we should not for precisely the same reasons continue to a further point, and then again to a further one, with no possibility of ever reaching a point at which we can properly rest. The real outcome of Hume's argument, therefore, is that 'antecedent scepticism' is illogical. The 'reliability of our faculties' cannot be the test of a proposition's probability. This point, I take it, is implicit in Hume's criticism, in the *Enquiry*, of Cartesian scepticism ('antecedent' scepticism); in the *Treatise*, however, he writes as if the regress were merely an infinite process which would come to a stop once all confidence in our beliefs was destroyed. And we can never regain that confidence, he then suggests, by any philosophical argument; we are saved only by a trick of our imagination. The philosophical 'refutation' of scepticism dismisses it in an 'expeditious way' as self-contradictory, on the ground that 'if the sceptical reasonings be strong, 'tis a proof that reason may have some force and authority; if weak, they can never be sufficient to invalidate all the conclusions of our understanding' (T, 186). But this refutation, Hume argues, cannot be sustained. The force of the sceptical arguments can only be diminished by correspondingly diminishing the authority of reason; and their force will only be totally destroyed at the point at which reason itself completely loses its authority. 'They both vanish away into nothing, by a regular and just diminution' (T, 187). So long as proof is possible, the sceptical position can be proved to be true; if proof is impossible, then the sceptical position can no longer be proved, but will be true. Thus, once again, the philosophical problem—in this case, the refutation of scepticism—is insoluble; the only soluble problem lies within the science of mind—why do the arguments of the sceptic, although they 'admit of no answer', yet 'produce no conviction'?

We are rescued from scepticism by 'a trivial property of the fancy'. The sceptical reasoning is too strained; as it proceeds from the reliability of '*p*' to the reliability of our faculties in investigating the reliability of our faculties . . . its propositions become ever more complicated and remote. Before long, they are quite incapable of capturing the full attention of the mind; in consequence, the sceptical idea in which our reasoning terminates will completely lack vividness. Were it not for the fact that 'belief is more properly an act of the sensitive, than of the cogitative part of our natures' (T, 183)—a matter of vividness as distinct from rational demonstration—scepticism would 'subvert all belief and opinion'. But, in fact, our irrationality preserves our Reason.

This argument is of considerable importance in establishing the sceptical mood of the *Treatise*; for it is to this particular 'trivial fancy' that Hume specifically refers when he wishes to show that we cannot without 'the most fatal consequences' rely upon 'the established', as distinct from 'the trivial', properties of the imagination. Yet, clearly, Hume is as unsuccessful at this point as he is elsewhere in substituting a psychological for a philosophical problem. Propositions like 'the understanding entirely subverts itself', 'we are saved by a trivial property of the fancy', 'belief is more properly a part of the sensitive than of the cogitative parts of our nature', are no more exempt from sceptical doubts than any other. Hume cannot really evade the traditional arguments against scepticism. He professes to *show* that reasoning and scepticism destroy one another simultaneously; but if reasoning be really destroyed, that argument, too, must collapse. Unless scepticism can be refuted, the science of man must be destroyed along with every other form of reasoning; but if reasoning is destroyed, there is no way of showing even that scepticism *cannot* be refuted or that reasoning *has been* destroyed.

In the *Enquiry*, whatever his motive, Hume makes no mention of this kind of scepticism; perhaps, as I suggested, he has noticed the difficulties to which it leads, perhaps he is merely made uncomfortable by the 'excessive scepticism' which temporarily subverted his main purposes in the *Treatise*. The Cartesian doubt is to be retained only in a 'moderate' and 'reasonable' sense, as a positive methodological principle. We ought, in the manner the Cartesian method suggests, 'to begin with clear and self-evident principles, to advance by timorous and sure steps, to review frequently our conclusions, and examine accurately all their consequences' (E, 150)—a passage which, with its verbal echoes of the *Discourse on Method*,[1] indicates the

---

[1] Part II; Vol. 1, p. 92. Hume may, of course, have read these rules in the *Port Royal Logic*, which quotes them at length (Pt. IV, Ch. i).

extent to which the Cartesian philosophy is now influential in his thinking.

The Cartesian scepticism about sensory perception—a type of 'consequent' scepticism—caused Hume no serious qualms. Scepticism, he says, may be carried so far that 'even our very senses are brought into dispute, by a certain species of philosophers; and the maxims of common life are subjected to the same doubt as the most profound principles or conclusions of metaphysics and theology' (E, 150). But the ordinary arguments (in the Cartesian manner) against the reliability of our senses show only that 'the senses alone are not implicitly to be depended on'. We must correct their evidence—for example, 'the crooked appearance of an oar in water'—by reason. However, 'there are other more profound arguments against the senses, which admit not of so easy a solution'.

These 'profound arguments' are, in general terms, Hume's *Scepticism with Regard to the Senses*, as that was presented in the *Treatise*. But his detailed theory of perception finds here no place, whether because it is too intricate for the *Enquiry*, or because its very elaborateness led Hume to suspect it. The sceptical, as distinct from the psychological, implications of his argument are now insisted upon. 'A blind and powerful instinct of Nature'—what Descartes called 'a certain spontaneous inclination'[1]—leads us to 'repose faith in our senses'. This instinct, however, would have us suppose 'the very images of the senses' to be external objects; were we uncritically to accept its promptings, we should never realize that images are 'nothing but representations'. The 'slightest philosophy', on the other hand, teaches us that 'nothing can ever be present to the mind but an image or perception, and that the senses are only the inlets, through which these images are conveyed'. To this extent, Reason compels us to reject the teachings of Instinct, and 'to embrace a new system with regard to the evidence of the senses'.

But how can this new system be justified? Certainly not by an appeal to the instincts of nature, since 'that led us to a quite different system, which is acknowledged fallible and even

[1] *Third Meditation*, Vol. 1, p. 160.

erroneous'. Nor is there even 'any appearance of argument' which can justify 'this pretended philosophical system'. At this point, for the first time, Hume sharply separates himself from the Cartesian system. There is no possible way of showing that our perceptions arise from external objects. 'The mind has never anything present to it but the perceptions, and cannot possibly reach any experience of their connexion with objects.' To 'have recourse to the veracity of the supreme Being', in the manner of the Cartesians,[1] 'in order to prove the veracity of our senses, is surely making a very unexpected circuit.' If God's veracity were involved, 'our senses would be entirely infallible'—and furthermore, 'if the external world be once called in question, we shall be at a loss to find arguments, by which we may prove the existence of that Being or any of his attributes' (E, 153).

On this matter, then, 'the profounder and more philosophical sceptics' will always triumph. The theory of representative perception, so Hume writes in the *Treatise*, is 'the monstrous offspring of two principles which are contrary to each other, which are both at once embrac'd by the mind, and which are unable mutually to destroy each other' (T, 215). The vitality of the theory derives just from this fact; it 'humours' both Reason and Instinct—Instinct, in allowing that external bodies exist; Reason, in denying that our perceptions are themselves external bodies. Yet neither Reason nor Instinct can be employed in its defence.

Not only does Reason now battle against Instinct, but Reason is even at odds with itself. For Reason, in the form of 'modern enquirers', tells us that secondary qualities are not, as primary qualities are, 'in the objects themselves'; but Reason can also prove that if secondary qualities are not in objects, primary qualities cannot be there either. In the *Treatise*—in that section entitled *Of the Modern Philosophy*—Hume's argument to this conclusion made use of his theory of space. On that theory, an 'extended object' is an arrangement of coloured or solid points. According to the 'modern philosophy', colour is nothing but a 'false idea' whereas solidity is an actual property of objects. But solidity, Hume argues, means impenetrability; to

[1] *Sixth Meditation*, Vol. 1, p. 191.

recognize a body as solid, therefore, we must be able to distinguish it from other bodies which fail to penetrate it. Such distinctions are impossible unless bodies have properties *other than* their solidity—and these other qualities can only be the so-called 'secondary qualities'. Thus, Hume concludes, 'there is a direct opposition . . . betwixt those conclusions we form from cause and effect, and those that persuade us of the continu'd and independent existence of body' (T, 231).

In the *Enquiry*, he cannot make use of his theory of space, which he omitted from that work. And he seems by now to have appreciated the force of Berkeley's reasoning, which he is content to summarize. 'If all the qualities, perceived by the senses, be in the mind, not in the object, the same conclusion must reach the idea of extension, which is wholly dependent on the sensible ideas or the ideas of secondary qualities' (E, 154). From this conclusion only *Abstraction* can save us— and Abstraction Berkeley has proved to be 'unintelligible and even absurd'. Thus, Hume concludes, 'the evidence of sense or the opinion of external existence' is actually *contrary* to reason—'at least, if it be a principle of reason, that all sensible qualities are in the mind not in the object'. For 'external existence' then reduces to the existence of 'a certain unknown, inexplicable *something*', which is 'a notion so imperfect, that no sceptic will think it worth while to contend against it' (E, 155).

Antitheses of this sort—Reason against Instinct, Reason against Sense, Reason against Reason—are, of course, a favourite sceptical device: in particular, Hume is here imitating the practice of Sextus Empiricus.[1] Berkeley thought he had

---

[1] Bayle's article on Pyrrho refers to Gassendi's *De fine logicae*, one part of which, *Modi Epoches Scepticorum circa Veritatem* (Opera omnia, Lugduni, 1658, Vol. i, p. 72) is a summary of the 'ten modes' of Pyrrhonian scepticism. According to Bayle, 'the name of Sextus Empiricus was scarcely known in the schools; what he proposed with so great subtilty concerning suspending one's judgment, was not less unknown here than the Terra Australis when Gassendus gave us an abridgment of it, which opened our eyes'. But there is some evidence to suggest that Sextus had been translated into English as early as 1590, although no copy of the translation is now extant, and Stanley's *History of Philosophy* (1665–62) contains a considerable segment of Sextus in translation. At least by the time he came to write the *Enquiry Concerning the Principles of Morals* (E, 180n), Hume could refer directly to Sextus' writings.

shown that 'the new philosophy' was quite untenable; while it prevailed, he argued, philosophers were naturally led into scepticism, but with its rejection, scepticism collapses.[1] The bulk of men are undisturbed by scepticism because they follow 'the dictates of Nature';[2] the philosopher can achieve the same freedom from sceptical qualms by ceasing to distinguish between ideas and things. If Hume had followed Berkeley, then there would have been no clash between Reason and Reason, or Reason and Sense.

But Hume refuses to accept Berkeley's answer to scepticism; in his eyes, 'the writings of that very ingenious author form the best lessons of scepticism, which are to be found either among the ancient or modern philosophers, Bayle not excepted' (E, 155n). Any theory is sceptical which questions 'sense', now identified with the belief in external, independent existence. Furthermore, Hume constantly employs that species of sceptical argument to which Berkeley particularly objected, the argument that 'the faculties we have are few, and those designed by nature for the support and pleasure of life, and not to penetrate into the inward essence and constitution of things';[3] with the aid of precisely this argument, Hume hopes to show that we have 'got quite beyond the reach of our faculties' when we 'carry our speculations . . . into the creation and formation of the universe' (D, 135). So far, he is quite prepared to accept and use for his own purposes the sort of scepticism to be found in the Port Royal logic, the scepticism sustained in the *Dialogues* by Demea.

As Berkeley pointed out, that scepticism depends for its force on the contrast between ideas (whose inward nature we *can* know) and things (whose inward nature lies forever concealed, just because we have no direct access to them). Hume might go so far with Berkeley as to argue that colours as well as shapes must be 'in the object'—this was essential to his theory of space—but he could not accept either Berkeley's view that things are ideas or the 'vulgar' view that ideas are

---

[1] *Principles*, § 86-9.
[2] *Op. cit.*, Introduction § 1.
[3] *Ibid.* § 2.

things.[1] He recognized the validity of Berkeley's arguments against representative perception but denied the truth of Berkeley's conclusion; he agreed with the 'vulgar' that we perceive things, but with 'the modern philosopher' that we are *directly* acquainted only with ideas. Thus Reason (i.e. 'modern philosophy') clashes with Reason (i.e. Berkeley's arguments); both forms of Reason are in opposition to Instinct (i.e. the opinion of the vulgar); and Reason in its Berkeleian form clashes with Sense. The distinction between ideas and things was one which did not fully satisfy either Reason or Instinct; yet Hume continues to believe that philosophy is committed to it. The outcome of such uncertainties is inevitably sceptical.

Much more serious, in Hume's eyes, is scepticism about Reason, which, in the *Enquiry*, takes the form of scepticism about Space and Time—on account of their importance in the 'science of quantity'—and Causality—the foundation of 'moral reasoning'. On Space and Time, Hume begins in the manner of Bayle. 'No priestly dogmas', Hume writes, 'ever shocked common sense more than the doctrine of the infinite divisibility of extension, with its consequences; as they are pompously displayed by all geometricians and metaphysicians, with a kind of triumph and exultation. . . . But what renders the matter more extraordinary, is, that these seemingly absurd opinions are supported by a chain of reasoning, the clearest and most natural; nor is it possible for us to allow the premises without admitting the consequences' (E, 156). Bayle had expressed the matter thus: 'We are doubtless highly obliged to the mathematics; they demonstrate the existence of what is contrary to the most evident notions of our intellect. . . . If these ideas [of extension] are false, deceitful, chimerical and illusory, is there a notion in our mind, which we ought not to take for a mere phantom or matter of distrust?'[2]

And yet, precisely at this point, Hume rebels against scepticism. He did not see how he could abandon the ordinary distinction between ideas and things, to whatever sceptical

---

[1] Whether this is a correct interpretation either of Berkeley or of the vulgar opinion is another matter; our concern is to present the problem as Hume saw it.   [2] Art. *Zeno*, Note I.

conclusions it led; but he could, and did, reject the ordinary doctrine of infinite divisibility, upon which the sceptical arguments against Reason particularly rested. This is the central purpose of the theory of space and time developed in the *Treatise*; in the *Enquiry* the main text merely states the sceptical case, but he adds a footnote to the effect that 'it seems to me not impossible to avoid these absurdities and contradictions, if it be admitted, that there is no such thing as abstract or general ideas, properly speaking' (Berkeley's influence, once more, is now strong); in the *Dialogues*, certainly, Philo emphasizes 'the contradictions which adhere to . . . extension, space, time, motion; and, in a word, quantity of all kinds, the object of the only science that can fairly pretend to any certainty or evidence' (D, 131)—but Philo is constructing an elaborate *argumentum ad hominem* against the theology of Demea, and must not be taken to be, at every point, the mouthpiece of Hume's opinions.

There are two reasons, closely connected with one another, why Hume is unwilling to accept a purely sceptical account of Space and Time. The first is that such an account formed part of the stock-in-trade of apologists for theology. Thus the Port Royal *Art of Thinking*, for example, recommended that every philosopher should study the paradoxes of divisibility, 'in order to check his presumption, and to take away from him the boldness which would lead him to oppose his feeble intelligence to the truths which the Church proposes to him, under the pretext that he cannot understand them'.[1] As against this sort of obscurantism, Hume stood for 'Reason'. 'It certainly concerns all lovers of science', he wrote, 'not to expose themselves to the ridicule and contempt of the ignorant by their conclusions' (E, 158n); and his tongue is not, as one might imagine, in his cheek. Secondly, as the quotation from the *Dialogues* makes particularly clear, Hume thought that uncertainties in the theory of space and time brought with them uncertainties in the whole 'science of quantity'. And he would not abate his claims for Reason, in its pure or 'demonstrative' or mathematical form. In that form, clear ideas are its subject matter; Hume

[1] Part IV, Ch. i.

143

is still enough of a Cartesian to be convinced that 'how any clear, distinct idea can contain circumstances, contradictory to itself, or to any other clear, distinct idea, is absolutely incomprehensible' (E, 157). It will not serve, now, to talk of 'difficulties'. 'A demonstration . . . is either irresistible, or has no manner of force. To talk therefore, of objections and replies, and balancing of arguments in such a question as this, is to confess, either that human reason is nothing but a play of words, or that the person himself, who talks so, has not a capacity equal to such subjects' (T, 31-32). Reason is a beacon in an uncertain world; if it were entirely extinguished, we should not even know what it is to be sceptical—to borrow a phrase from Hegel, 'in the night all cows are black'.

But 'moral' reasoning cannot, by the same methods, be preserved inviolate. As in the case of scepticism about the senses, this sort of scepticism, Hume says, may take either a 'popular' or a 'philosophical' form. 'Popular' scepticism insists on 'the natural weakness of the human understanding', or points to 'the variations of our judgement'. But it is soon dispelled; for we cannot *help* reasoning—'we reason every moment concerning matter of fact and existence'—a fact which is, by itself, sufficient to destroy all 'popular objections' to moral reasoning. The sceptic, therefore, ought to keep within his proper, *philosophical*, sphere, emphasizing those objections which arise from his 'more profound researches' (in other words, from Hume's theory of causality). These researches have proved that all 'moral reasoning' rests on nothing 'but custom or a certain instinct of our nature; which it is indeed difficult to resist, but which, like other instincts, may be fallacious and deceitful' (E, 159). The effect of this discovery, Hume goes on to suggest, is 'to destroy all assurance and conviction'. His theory of causality, we are now given to understand, is a variety of Pyrrhonian or 'excessive' scepticism; if we were to take it seriously, 'all discourse, all action would immediately cease; and men remain in a total lethargy, till the necessities of nature, unsatisfied, put an end to their miserable existence' (E, 160). If these calamitous consequences do not in fact beset the sceptic, this is only because 'Nature' steps in, and prevents us from regarding our 'doubts and scruples' as anything but 'a mere amusement', with no effect but 'to show the whimsical condition of mankind, who must act and reason and believe; though they are not able, by their most diligent enquiry, to satisfy themselves concerning the foundations of these operations, or to remove the objections, which may be raised against them' (E, 160).

Hume's scepticism at this point is thoroughly Cartesian. It is not on the face of it at all obvious why the discovery that we can never *show* that 'objects which have, in our experience, been frequently conjoined, will likewise, in other instances, be conjoined in the same manner' should plunge us into a 'total lethargy'. We discover that no 'general rule' will justify our causal inferences; must we therefore decide to give up predicting? Our beliefs, we now find, are 'part of our sensitive nature'; does it follow that we should, if we took this theory seriously, give up believing? Hume has certainly in the back of his mind the Cartesian dictum that 'only those objects should engage our attention, to the sure and indubitable knowledge of which our mental powers seem to be adequate'.[1] In the *Treatise*, similarly, he writes as follows: 'it is our aim in all our studies and reflections' to discover 'that energy in the cause, by which it operates on its effect; that tie, which connects them together; and that efficacious quality, on which the tie depends' (T, 266). If this were true, then certainly Hume's theory of causality must lead us to abandon 'all study and reflection'; but that it is true is an assumption which Boyle and Newton had already questioned. In speaking as if his theory of causality would, without the special intervention of 'Nature', destroy all action, Hume is certainly exaggerating the extent of his scepticism; it would not even destroy science—except in so far as it rests on a theory of discrete particulars, as distinct from genuine 'constant conjunctions'—although it would certainly destroy certain 'scientific' ambitions (the quest for 'rational connections' and the quest for 'certainty'). Hume

---

[1] *Regulae*, II. I do not mean to imply, of course, that Hume had actually read the *Regulae*. This passage conveniently summarizes the characteristic Cartesian doctrine.

does not adequately distinguish what is *genuinely* sceptical in his theory from what is sceptical only in the eyes of a rationalist.

How precisely can 'Nature' save us from scepticism? In this appeal to Nature, Hume is a child of his age: and yet his *Dialogues on Natural Religion* were specifically directed against the idea of Nature, as his age most often understood it—as a single orderly design.[1] Furthermore, the *Enquiry* does not make quite that use of Nature which we might at first expect; Hume was not, in the full sense, a naturalist. He nowhere suggests that causality must be reliable *because it rests upon Instinct*. Reason is 'nothing but a wonderful and unintelligible instinct in our souls' (T, 179), but Hume does not conclude, as Pope would, that it is all the better for being an instinct. The *Essay on Man* is naturalism in its unmitigated form:

> Say, where full instinct is the unerring guide,
> What pope or council can they need beside?
>
> .   .   .   .   .   .
>
> Sure ne'er to o'ershoot, but just to hit;
> While still too wide or short is human wit;
> Sure by quick nature happiness to gain,
> Which heavier reason labours at in vain.
> This too serves always, reason never long;
> One must go right, the other may go wrong.[2]

Had Hume been prepared to take this view, Beattie would have found in him an ally, not an enemy. Beattie admonishes us that 'it were well if we laid our systems aside, and were more attentive in observing those impulses of Nature in which reason has no part'[3] and sees nothing sceptical in the assertion that 'I account that to be truth which the constitution of my nature determines me to believe'.[4] But this *theological* conception of Nature plays no part in Hume's thinking.

At one stage in the *Enquiry*—the section entitled *The Sceptical Solution of These Doubts*—we might well imagine that Hume is working towards this, the naturalist reply to scepticism. 'It is more conformable to the ordinary wisdom of nature to secure

---

[1] cf. C. L. Becker, *The Heavenly City of the Eighteenth-Century Philosophers* (Ch. 2).   [2] *Epistle III*, lines 83-94.
[3] *Essay on Truth*, p. 64.   [4] *Ibid.*, p. 35.

so necessary an act of the mind [causal inference], by some instinct or mechanical tendency, which may be infallible in its operations' (E, 55). But this remark occurs in a context of piety, which by itself makes us suspicious: 'those who delight in the discovery and contemplation of final causes', he writes, 'have here ample subject to employ their wonder and declamation.' And the rather awkward phrase—'which *may be* infallible'— presages Hume's final conclusion; Hume does not want to say 'which *is* infallible', and yet also he does not wish, too soon, to rule out this possibility. His final conclusion, however, is that reason 'like other instincts, may be fallacious or deceitful' (E, 159). If instinct can so far deceive us that we are led to imagine 'our very perceptions' to be external objects, how can we possibly place any reliance on it?

Instinct, then, cannot save us from scepticism; the 'Nature' which intervenes is simply *our own nature*, which is incapable of taking sceptical arguments with any seriousness. Bayle had made a similar point: 'There never was and never will be', he wrote, 'but a small number of men capable of being deceived by the arguments of the sceptics. . . . The natural inclination men have to be peremptory [is] an impenetrable shield against the darts of the Pyrrhonists'.[1] This 'natural inclination men have to be peremptory' becomes in Hume's *Treatise* 'careless-ness and inattention' (T, 218); in the *Enquiry* it is 'action and employment and the occupations of common life' (E, 159). We are incapable, for reasons which are purely psychological, of taking Pyrrhonism seriously. 'A Stoic or Epicurean displays principles, which may not only be durable, but which have an effect on conduct and behaviour. But a Pyrrhonian cannot expect that his philosophy will have any constant influence on the mind' (E, 160). This does not show that Pyrrhonism is false—practical consequences are not, for Hume, a criterion of truth—but only that it is untenable. To tell us not to pass judgments because they may be false is to give us advice which we cannot possibly take—'Nature, by an absolute and uncon-troulable necessity has determin'd us to judge as well as to breathe and feel' (T, 183).

[1] Art. *Pyrrho*.

147

Similarly, there is no point in telling us that we ought not to believe in the existence of external bodies. 'Nature has not left this to [our] choice, and has doubtless esteem'd it an affair of too great importance to be trusted to our uncertain reasonings and speculations. We may well ask, *What causes induce us to believe in the existence of body?* but 'tis in vain to ask *Whether there be body or not?* That is a point, which we must take for granted in all our reasonings' (T, 187). If we interpret this passage literally, we shall certainly see objections to it, those objections which H. H. Price has particularly emphasized.[1] Hume is asserting, on the face of it, that it is psychologically impossible to doubt whether bodies exist; yet he admits (T, 217) that he himself feels doubt on the matter, even if the doubt does not last very long; and, indeed, unless this doubt were possible, our belief in the existence of bodies would not genuinely be a *belief*—we do not 'believe' what it is quite impossible to question. Hume must really mean, Price thinks, that 'Do bodies exist?' is a question which it is *logically* impossible to pose. 'This interrogative formula, though grammatically correct, does not formulate a question at all. (Compare the interrogative formula "how many miles is it from here to the middle of last week?")'

But Price's interpretation is certainly not Hume's meaning: the question 'how many miles is it from here to the middle of next week?' is one to which no answer makes sense, whereas Hume clearly thinks that it makes perfect sense to assert that bodies *do* exist, although 'it is in vain to assert' that they *do not* exist. His meaning, with the reference to 'Nature' interpreted, as it must be, in psychological terms, is that no one can seriously (regularly or consistently) maintain that bodies do not exist. Sceptical arguments can throw us into 'momentary amazement, irresolution and confusion' (E, 155n), in which we are 'inviron'd with the deepest darkness, and utterly depriv'd of the use of every member and faculty' (T, 269), but these, we discover from experience, do not endure. Nature saves us, then, not because its promptings are infallible—on the contrary, they are known to be fallible—but because our own nature

[1] *Hume's Theory of the External World*, pp. 11-12.

148

prevents us from taking our own reasonings with any real seriousness. We cannot keep to a resolution to follow Reason, although, equally, we cannot consistently follow Nature. Either policy will lead us into confusion and contradiction. 'I know not what ought to be done in the present case. I can only observe what is commonly done; which is, that this difficulty is seldom or never thought of; and even where it has once been present to the mind, is quickly forgot, and leaves but a small impression behind it' (T, 268). And what is commonly done, we philosophers shall also do, not because we want to, or because we ought to, but just because this is how we are made. The 'answer' to scepticism is not a philosophical argument but a psychological fact.

Obviously, this doctrine can easily lead to obscurantism and Philistinism. If, after all our reasonings, we must in the end return to the indifference which 'the vulgar' achieve without the trouble of thinking, what is the point of philosophizing? If it be true that when 'we believe, that fire burns, or water refreshes' this is 'only because it costs us too much pains to think otherwise' (T, 270), does it not follow that one pleasing belief is quite as good as another? The sceptic, says Philo in the *Dialogues*, 'must act, and live, and converse like other men; and for this conduct he is not obliged to give any other reason than the absolute necessity he lies under of so doing' (D, 134); but he is not, one might reply, compelled by the same necessity to philosophize—why undertake so troublesome a pursuit? Hume's first answer is that it is not troublesome, at least to those with a taste for it. Should he himself abandon philosophy for other pursuits he would be 'a loser in point of pleasure'; and this, he says, 'is the origin of my philosophy' (T, 271). Some people *like* philosophizing; that, whatever the severer moralists may say, is in itself a justification for philosophizing.

But this is not the whole of Hume's answer: it is the answer to which Pyrrhonism drives him, but he adds to it a more general justification. 'We must submit to this fatigue, in order to live at ease ever after' (E, 12). Like Epicurus, he thought that we had need of philosophy in so far as it helped to free us from superstition. 'I make bold to recommend philosophy, and shall not scruple to give it the preference over superstition of every kind or denomination' (T, 271). Men, by nature, pass beyond that 'narrow circle of subjects, which are the subject of daily conversation and action'; and beyond that circle philosophy is a far better guide than religion, if only because it will 'seldom go so far as to interrupt the course of our natural propensities' (T, 272).

What sort of philosophy should we choose as our guide? Certainly not 'metaphysics', which is merely an ally of superstition (E, 12). And Pyrrhonism cannot be our guide, because it leads us nowhere. What we need is a theory with enough of Pyrrhonism in it to preserve us from dogmatism, but not enough to drive us into inaction. And such a 'mitigated scepticism' Hume thought he could discern in the 'New Academy': the scepticism which derived from the teachings of Philo, the scepticism which Hume's 'Philo' teaches in the Dialogues, and which Hume himself briefly sketches in the Enquiry.

Such a mitigated scepticism will make us tolerant of others, for it insists that 'there is a degree of doubt, and caution, and modesty, which, in all kinds of scrutiny and decision, ought for ever to accompany a just reasoner' (E, 162). But, more than that—and in this way it fits in with Hume's major programme —it will direct our attention 'to such enquiries as are best adapted to the narrow capacity of the human understanding'. The imagination of man, unless in some way subdued, is 'delighted with whatever is remote and extraordinary, running, without control, into the most distant parts of space and time in order to avoid the objects, which custom has rendered too familiar to it'. Once we are thoroughly convinced of 'the force of the Pyrrhonian doubt', we shall no longer be tempted 'to go beyond common life'—our philosophy will contain nothing but 'the reflections of common life, methodized and corrected'. And these systematized reflections are the science of man. 'So long as we confine our speculations to trade, or morals, or politics, or criticism, we make appeals, every moment, to common sense and experience, which strengthen our philosophical conclusions, and remove (at least, in part) the suspicion, which we so justly entertain with regard to every reasoning that is very subtle and refined' (D, 135). Beyond these fields, into the cosmogonies of theology or into that 'world of its own' (T, 271) which superstition constructs, the mind which has been chastened by scepticism will never move. 'While we cannot give a satisfactory reason, why we believe, after a thousand experiments, that a stone will fall, or fire burn: can we ever satisfy ourselves concerning any determination, which we may form, with regard to the origin of worlds, and the situation of nature from, and to, eternity?' (E, 162).

This, then, is the conclusion which most effectively satisfies Hume's diverse intentions. Science is saved: scepticism brings with it, not only freedom from superstition, but, more positively, an interest in the 'right kind' of science—science which is either mathematical (that ever-present 'exceptional case') or else 'moral' (with physics perhaps permitted entry, but a subdued physics, quite without pretensions to superiority); and beyond science there lies nothing whatsoever. But scepticism constantly moved beyond its subordinate role, threatening the security of the social sciences, undermining common sense as well as metaphysics, opening the gates so wide to arbitrariness that the metaphysician could ride in as freely as the scientist. Hume could not succeed in the impossible —a science founded on scepticism no degree of ingenuity can successfully construct.

HUME'S ACHIEVEMENT

HUME's reputation was not easily won: in England, it dates back only to the last decades of the nineteenth century. And, even now, he has his detractors. A. E. Taylor doubted whether Hume is a great philosopher—'a very clever man' is the utmost concession he would allow.[1] But this is mild criticism compared with Prichard's downright denunciation: 'The *Treatise*', he wrote, 'is one of the most tedious of books, and close examination of it renders me not sceptical but angry. Of course, there is a great deal of cleverness in it, but the cleverness is only that of extreme ingenuity or perversity, and the ingenuity is only exceeded by the perversity. . . . It could be wished that the student of philosophy could be spared all contact with Hume, and thereby the trouble of rooting out some of the more gratuitous forms of confusion common to philosophy.'[2]

Hume certainly had an ingenious mind: he took such delight in reconciling apparent exceptions with his hypotheses that the very ingenuity with which this is done tells against him. 'Cleverness', in the dyslogistic sense of the word, is a not inadequate description of Hume at his worst. One must add, however, that the *Treatise* is much more subject to this defect than the *Enquiry*; 'cleverness' is an undergraduate vice, and Hume largely conquers it, as not every philosopher has succeeded in doing. But Hume's mind, even at its best, was not of the most disciplined sort. Rigour and consistency were not his strong points, and these are qualities which we ordinarily expect from a great philosopher.

On the other side, philosophical rigour is sometimes difficult to distinguish from *rigor mortis*; Hume is genuinely speculative, genuinely experimental, with no inclination to set up axioms or to construct deductive systems. If he is so often led into

---

[1] 'Hume on the Miraculous' (*Philosophical Studies*, p. 365).

[2] *Knowledge and Perception*, p. 174.

inconsistencies, or into tortuous and implausible ingenuities, this is partly because he has a real respect for facts; he is never tempted to dismiss exceptions as 'appearances'. We are always conscious, in reading Hume, of a philosophical mind actively at work; and, to an unusual degree, he 'shows his hand'. We never feel, as we sometimes do when studying other philosophers, that his philosophy is no more than a defensive system, depending for its force on principles which are extrinsic to it—on moral and religious attitudes which the philosopher is scrupulous not to mention, but which are yet the sole conceivable 'justification' of the system he is erecting.

Was Hume's achievement 'purely negative'? This, the common way of putting the question, arises out of the assumption that 'negative' is a deprecatory expression, that a 'negative' philosopher must be inferior to a 'positive' one. But this is not so: to show that some plausible position is untenable is itself an achievement, whereas a 'positive' philosophy may do no more than add another to the already tedious aggregation of wilful fantasies. If all that can be said in Hume's favour is that he showed (even unconsciously, as the legend has it) that the theory of ideas could never give an account of ordinary perception, this would be in itself a lesson worth teaching, one still not universally taken to heart.

But what philosophers have failed to realize is that the *Treatise* is an attack on *philosophy*, at least as that subject was ordinarily conceived. It is one of the ironies of history that Hume woke Kant from his 'dogmatic slumber' only so far as to inspire him to construct the very kind of philosophical system to which Hume most objected. And epistemologists are still, in Hume's honour, constructing systems in which independent things are magically evolved out of perceptions. The penetrating power of Hume's critique has no doubt been weakened by the unacceptability of the alternatives he proposed: the philosophic spirit can never be satisfied with a 'cure for scepticism' which consists in no more than 'carelessness and inattention'. But, as well, his achievements have been seriously misread; as when he has been thought to be contributing to an epistemology which he has in fact rejected as a mere confusion, as either psychology or nothing. It has even been supposed that, by some misfortune, he failed 'to distinguish philosophical problems from psychological ones' or that, by an oversight, 'he never quite succeeded in drawing the distinction which Kant later drew between the Transcendental Imagination and the Empirical Imagination'.[1] In short, it has been objected against Hume that he failed to do precisely what, so he deliberately argued, never could be done. What Kant said of Hume's critics—'they were ever assuming what he doubted, and demonstrating with eagerness and even with arrogance what he never thought of disputing'[2]—still remains true, and as applicable to Kant as to anyone else.

One may, I should say one must, reject Hume's attempt to displace philosophy by psychology; but there is no use trying to continue with the *kind* of philosophy which he particularly showed to be unstable, and this, oddly enough, is precisely what his admirers have so often done. A philosophy which does not *sharply* distinguish itself from psychology, or a philosophy which conceives its task as that of making science 'safe', can never 'answer Hume'. Hume's great achievement, although, in his Cartesian moods, he was himself somewhat alarmed by it, lies in his contribution to a quite different conception of science, in which speculation, not security, is the key-note, in which science can no longer preen itself on its superiority to 'imagination', but just for that reason appears in its true colours, as a form of human enterprise.

The two main lessons in logic which Hume had to teach are succinctly expressed in his *Dialogues on Natural Religion*—and freed, there, from psychological accretions. The first is that 'there is an evident absurdity in pretending to demonstrate a matter of fact' (D, 189); in other words, it is always logically possible for an empirical proposition to be false. The second is that 'every event, before experience, is equally difficult and incomprehensible; and every event, after experience, is equally easy and intelligible' (D, 182). In other words, intelligibility is no more than familiarity; there is no total

[1] *Hume's Theory of the External World* (H. H. Price), p. 15.
[2] *Prolegomena to any Future Metaphysic* (trans. Mahaffy and Bernard), p. 5.

scheme of things, no rational order, by reference to which we can see—or could see, were our faculties more powerful—that what happens could not intelligibly happen otherwise. An hypothesis is intelligible if, and only if, we have had previous experience of the kind of connexion to which it points; we come to accept it as true, not because we discover that it *must* be true, but because, in various ways, it 'grows on us'. And in our acceptance of it, there is always an element of commitment. It is in this sense that belief is 'more properly a part of the sensitive than of the cogitative part of our nature.'

Hume is a critic, then, both of rationalism in its classical form and of that theory of science as pure experience which often goes under the name of 'empiricism'. Empirical knowledge can never be deduced *a priori*, nor is it reducible to a collocation of perceptions. But Hume does not quite shake himself free from the Cartesian tradition. There is something, he insists, about which we cannot be mistaken: what lies directly before us —impressions and ideas, and the relations of contiguity and resemblance which hold between them. He hopes to preserve inviolate the certainty of mathematics, as a 'relation between ideas' which makes no reference to 'external existence' (E, 25); and to preserve, also, the certainty of the science of man in so far as that science merely describes what our mind contains. And then the ordinary world begins to look *peculiarly* doubtful, uncertain, fraught with insecurity, in contrast with the internal world of impressions and ideas. There is nothing to induce scepticism in the mere fact that our beliefs might be false, unless we look at that fact from the vantage-point of a security which is absolute; and Hume often falls into this sort of scepticism, this perverted rationalism, just because the theory of ideas gives him such a vantage-point. But it was still a great achievement to demolish that other world picture, which drives us into scepticism by contrasting the tentative successes, the 'mere hypotheses', of science with an intrinsically intelligible knowledge, with which, it is supposed, a God-like scientist would wholly concern himself.

Of course, Hume's assault on rationalism has not proved altogether successful; even the theory of design is still with us.

This is not surprising. Men cling to the ideal of an utterly secure science just as they do to the ideal of an utterly secure world: Utopia still exerts its fascination. But, as well, Hume's allegiance to the theory of ideas considerably weakened the force of his argument; and, to make matters worse, he was committed to a species of nominalism. 'Perceptions', as well as being transparent, are also 'particular', general only in so far as they resemble one another. This reduction of universality to resemblance, however amenable it may be to Hume's associationist designs, considerably weakens the force of his logic. It is obviously not true, for example, that a cause is 'an object, followed by another, and where all the objects similar to the first are followed by objects similar to the second' (E, 76); a person who asserts that a disease is caused by the entrance of a certain virus into the body is not committed to saying that anything which is in any way similar to the entrance of that virus (e.g. the entry of a different virus) will give rise to a similar disease. Hume's nominalism, in fact, makes it impossible for him to give any account of regularity. Experience, as he describes it, is 'loose and separate', not merely in the sense (vital to an anti-rationalist philosophy) that it is not a system of mutual implications, but also in the sense that it consists wholly of what is merely particular; thus Hume inevitably provokes a rationalist reaction, the leaders of which could plausibly profess or speak in the name of science, as the defenders of generality.

In spite, however, of these defects, Hume was a logician of the first importance; whereas as a psychologist, for all the prominence of the 'science of man' in his writings, his work is of the slightest consequence. One could, without any scruples, write a history of psychology which made no mention of Hume; whereas one could not omit Hartley. And yet both set out to be the Newton of 'the science of man'; and both found in associationism the clue to that science. Wherein lies the difference?

The fact is that just because Hume tries to turn logic into psychology, he does not see what a psychological issue is like; by trying to make psychology the *scientia scientiarum* he destroys it as a science. Once again he is misled by Cartesianism; the theory of ideas not only provokes that endless series of epistemological constructions which has so seriously diverted philosophy from its real task, it also perpetuated that confusion between philosophical and psychological questions from which we are still suffering. It led Hume to suppose that he was engaging in 'mental geography', by delineating 'the distinct parts and powers of the mind' (E, 13); he thought he was confronted by a set of 'internal' objects, which could be classified just in the kind of way we classify geographical regions, when he was actually discussing what it means to be real, or in what the evidence for a scientific proposition consists. 'Every belief is associated with a present impression' is not really parallel, as Hume thought it was, to 'every valley is associated with a fault'; it does not assert that a certain connexion holds between 'internal objects'; it means that a proposition of science is always based upon observation. His theory of belief, as it at present stands, is an amalgam of psychology and logic; but we can cut away the psychology and leave a logic behind, whereas what is left as 'psychology' is the mere commonplace that believing is somehow different from imagining.

This is the crucial point of difference between Hume and Hartley. Hartley, too, is the victim of Cartesianism; but it is the *logic* in Hartley which (for the most part) is commonplace, and the psychology which is novel. When we read Hartley, we constantly encounter hypotheses which we can test by the ordinary processes of psychological enquiry—as when, for example, he develops his view about the way in which we learn to speak. Hartley describes the way in which people behave, distinguishing between the behaviour of this and that kind of person, and that is the psychological importance of his work. Hume's work, in contrast, does not incite us to undertake further psychological enquiry. His 'experiments' (T, 332) are utterly artificial; they are not science, but scientism. A genuine experiment is exploratory: Hume's 'experiments' are elaborate ways of asserting such commonplaces as that we are only proud of what is of some consequence. A genuine experiment confirms a hypothesis in some unexpected place: Hume's 'experiments' give us no reason for preferring associationism to any other *ad hoc* account of the workings of pride. They are illustrations, merely, and have not the force of a genuine experiment.

To make sense of Hume's theories, indeed, we must read 'things' for 'impressions', and 'empirical propositions' for 'beliefs'; it is things which are constantly conjoined; it is propositions, not 'ideas', which are 'associated with' the observations we have made. At the same time, Hume was perfectly right, I should say, in arguing that we cannot give a complete account of the workings of science by means of logical notions alone. If it be asked, for example, why a certain hypothesis is regarded as 'established' and another as 'doubtful', the answer can never be given in merely formal terms (e.g. by saying that the one hypothesis had led to more true conclusions than the other). Constant conjunction, as Hume saw, is necessary, but is not sufficient, to explain our acceptance (when we are thinking scientifically) of an hypothesis. If in the attempt to keep science 'pure' and 'rational', we try to exclude the effects of special interests, prevailing modes of thought, the desire to get on with a job, we destroy its vitality; and we are confronted with a mechanism of confirmation which seems quite inadequate for the task it has yet so successfully performed. Hume's successors thought he had shown the need for formulating 'an inductive logic'; but what he really showed is that there is not such a logic. He was wrong in concluding that logic played no part in scientific reasoning—wrong in thinking that science must be either demonstrative or inductive—but he was right in insisting that scientific thinking cannot be described as a simple application of logic. His theory of the imagination is crude and misleading, but his insistence upon the importance of the imagination as a co-partner to observation at every stage in our thinking contains a lesson we have yet fully to appreciate. A crude positivism, a phenomenalistic 'empiricism', is quite alien to the spirit of Hume's philosophy.

At the same time, of course, no small part of Hume's achievement was his critique of metaphysics. Metaphysics, in the transcendental sense, is 'not properly a science' (E, 11); and 'science' has not its narrower modern connotation but means 'body of knowledge'. The metaphysician either says nothing at all, or else what he says is not transcendental but empirical. As we have seen, the force of Hume's positivism is weakened by his allegiance to the doctrine of impressions and ideas and his consequent inability to give any precise account of what he means by 'resting upon experience'. But it is still clear enough in the *Treatise* and clearer in the *Dialogues on Natural Religion* just how powerful was Hume's attack on metaphysics. The *Dialogues* take the argument for design *seriously*, and Hume is able to show that although it purports to be an argument from experience, it is unable to point to any circumstances which would be incompatible with quite different hypotheses about the way things come into being: it cannot show that anything whatsoever would be different were the world *not* designed. And herein lies proof of its emptiness.

Hume's achievement, then, must be diversely described; his philosophy will not fit neatly with any of the ordinary categories. He is pre-eminently a breaker of new ground: a philosopher who opens up new lines of thought, who suggests to us an endless variety of philosophical explorations. No one could be a Humean, in the sense in which he could be a Hegelian; to be a Humean, precisely, is to take no system as final, nothing as ultimate except the spirit of enquiry.

HUME AND THE ETHICS OF BELIEF[1]

HUME is generally included among those who specifically deny that we can in any way choose what we shall believe. And with good warrant in the text. Consider, for example, the *reductio* argument which Hume employs in his Appendix to the *Treatise* (T, 623-4). He is there concerned to refute the view that a belief is distinguishable from other ideas in virtue of its having 'some new idea, such as that of *reality* or *existence*' annexed to it. And his argument runs thus: 'The mind has command over all its ideas, and can separate, unite, mix and vary them as it pleases; so that if belief consisted merely in a new idea, annex'd to the conception, it wou'd be in a man's power to believe what he pleas'd'. The argument ends at that point, the *reductio* is complete. In other words, Hume presumes it to be an obviously absurd doctrine that a man has the power to believe what he pleases. Any theory of belief which leaves open this possibility can at once, he is arguing, be dismissed. One can easily enough find other passages in Hume's writings to a similar effect. That belief is something that happens to us, rather than something we do, is implicit in his observation that '*belief is more properly an act of the sensitive, than of the cogitative part of our natures*' (T, 183). The supposition that we can believe what we please is, he more directly tells us, 'contrary to what we find by daily experience' (E, 48).

Enough, it might well be thought, has been said. Hume's position in respect to belief and decision is, to an unusual degree, indisputable. Yet, dipping into Hume, scholars have sometimes supposed him to take quite the contrary view. 'A wise man', they read in Hume's *Enquiry Concerning the Human Understanding*, 'proportions his belief to the evidence' (E, 110). Surely 'proportioning' is a cogitative act, if any-

---

[1] This Appendix is an extensively revised version of a paper delivered at the conference held in Edinburgh in 1976 to commemorate the bicentenary of Hume's death. I could not, of course, presume that my listeners had read *Hume's Intentions*; some repetition of what I have argued in the previous chapters is therefore inevitable. But not, I hope, to an intolerable degree.

thing is! And is not Hume, when he writes that sentence, exhorting us to decide not to believe until we have examined the evidence—as if we had the power, at least, to *suspend* our belief? If this be so, if we can sometimes choose not to believe, does it not follow that belief is in some measure under our control?

After all, we might add, it is one thing to say that we cannot choose to believe at will, if what this means is that we cannot, in respect to each and every proposition, decide whether to believe it or not to believe it. It is quite another thing to say that in *no* circumstances can we decide whether or not to believe a proposition. The first view, one can agree with Hume, is quite contrary to experience, so much so that I doubt whether any philosopher has ever seriously held it, although some philosophers have certainly written as if they did. If the rain is pelting down, I cannot simply decide to believe that it is not raining, any more than, Dostoevsky to the contrary notwithstanding, I can simply decide to believe that $2+2=5$. But it does not follow that when the evidence is inconclusive as between p and q I cannot decide to believe p rather than q, that the judge's 'I have decided to believe you' or the friend's 'I refuse to believe he could act in that way' are not to be taken literally. This is the only point that is really in dispute— whether Hume ever admits, as Locke does admit, that there are *some* circumstances in which belief is voluntary.[1]

Of the commentators on Hume, Price, for one, argues as much.[2] Or he argues at least that there are places in which Hume's philosophical procedures make sense only on the assumption that belief can sometimes be under our control. Hume's philosophical practice, on Price's view, is to that extent inconsistent with his mechanical theory of belief. A more straightforward inconsistency, as we have already noted, is at least suggested by Hume's observation that 'the wise man proportions his belief to the evidence'. So for all

---

[1] Compare J. A. Passmore: 'Locke and the Ethics of Belief', *Proceedings of the British Academy*, 1978, for Locke on this theme.
[2] H. H. Price: *Belief*, London, 1969, pp. 239-40.

that our initial tendency is to think of Hume as an exceptionally whole-hearted proponent of the view that we believe as we must, it is worth exploring the matter a little further—the more especially as, if there is a degree of tension in our ordinary thinking on this question, we might expect to find it reflected, like most other such tensions, in Hume's philosophy. And that there is such a tension is strongly suggested by the fact that while some philosophers tell us that it is logically impossible, incompatible with the very nature of belief, to suppose that we can ever choose to believe p rather than q, other philosophers take our power to do so to be self-evident—as we all seem to do when we so unselfconsciously use such phrases as 'I like to believe', 'I cannot bring myself to believe', 'my present inclination is to believe'.[1]

Let us begin by looking once more at Hume's theory of belief. One thing that surprises us at the outset is that Hume should so obviously think of himself as a pioneer. No one else, he tells us, has even suspected that there is any difficulty in determining in what belief consists (T, 628). We are surprised because Locke, to say nothing of such of his predecessors as Plato, had talked about belief at considerable length, even if sometimes, like Hume himself, under the name of assent. Hume would seek to dissipate our surprise by arguing that neither Locke nor Plato had supposed there to be any difficulty attaching to the act of believing as such—it was an act of the understanding and no more need be said. He himself was the first to anatomize the act of believing, as distinct from 'placing' belief epistemologically in its relation to knowledge.

Consider, in this light, Locke's definition of belief: 'The admitting or receiving [of] any proposition for true, upon arguments or proofs that are found to persuade us to receive it as true, without certain knowledge that it is so' (*Essay*, IV, xv, 3). Hume would object to this definition on three grounds: the first, that vague phrases like 'the admitting', 'the receiving'

[1] Compare, for example, Bernard Williams: *Problems of the Self* (Cambridge, 1973) with Descartes: *Principles of Philosophy* (Pt. 1, Principle XXXIV) or J. H. Newman: *An Essay in Aid of a Grammar of Assent* (New York, repr. 1955, p. 189).

conceal the fact that we are not being told in what *believing* consists as a psychological phenomenon; the second, that to define belief as admitting or receiving a proposition as true upon *arguments or proofs* wrongly suggests that our beliefs are all of them the conclusions of arguments; the third, that the phrase 'admitting or receiving'—'receiving' has here the same force as in 'the Ambassador received the guests'—makes it appear that we believe as we do only after scrutiny, whereas in fact our beliefs are automatic responses to particular forms of experience.

Hume can properly think of himself as an innovator, then, in at least two respects. First, in defining 'belief' in purely psychological terms, as a vivid perception rather than, along with Plato and Locke, as a proposition we hold to be true on evidence less than sufficient to demonstrate its truth and, secondly, in denying that beliefs necessarily or normally have their source in argument or deliberation.

We can see at once how sharply Hume differs from his predecessors by looking at the initial account of belief he presents in his second, considerably revised, discussion of 'the senses and the memory'. 'The *belief* or *assent* which always attends the memory and senses', he there informs us, 'is nothing but the vivacity of those perceptions they present . . .' (T, 86). Locke had argued that the senses give us knowledge; Hume will have none of this—they offer us beliefs, the belief that something is the case. And this has the consequence that a belief can have all the immediacy, although not the infalli-bility, of an intuition; it need not rest, anymore than for Locke knowledge need rest, on arguments or proofs. The whole process of coming to believe is spontaneous, completely in-voluntary; a vivid perception is at once a sensation or a memory and a belief. The belief 'attends' our memory and senses not as an inference from them but as an aspect of them. And this is still true, he later argues, even when the belief depends for its existence on a constant conjunction of experi-ences, as distinct from a single experience. 'The belief, which attends the present impression, and is produc'd by a number of past impressions and conjunctions . . . arises immediately, without any new operation of the reason or imagination' (T, 102). Our belief that it is raining outside is not a conclusion that we draw by a special process of inference from our previous experience that a particular sort of sound accompanies rain; it is something we *have as a result of that experience.*

Further to point the contrast between Hume and Locke, we can draw attention to the fact that in Locke's account of belief two distinct factors have always to be kept in mind. First, the objective probability of the proposition to which we give our assent; secondly, the degree of assurance we attach to that proposition. Ideally, and in large part in fact, those two are proportionate one to another. When they are not, this is because we get our calculations wrong: 'the foundation of error will lie in wrong measures of probability' (*Essay*, IV, xx, 16). How such errors can arise, how men can be so attached to false beliefs, is a question that deeply troubles Locke; he tries to explain such perversity in a variety of ways. But in every case, certainly, the degree of probability is one thing, the degree of assurance quite another.

In a familiar passage, Hume sweeps aside Locke's Janus-like analysis, and with it all Locke's problems about how degrees of assurance can come to be dissociated from degrees of probability. 'Thus all probable reasoning', he writes, 'is nothing but a species of sensation. 'Tis not solely in poetry and music, we must follow our taste and sentiment, but likewise in philosophy. When I am convinc'd of any principle, 'tis only an idea, which strikes more strongly upon me. When I give the preference to one set of arguments above another, I do nothing but decide from my feeling concerning the superiority of their influence' (T, 103). This makes it look as if Locke's problem—how we can have a degree of assurance which is not conformable to the probabilities—ought not, for Hume, so much as arise. The question makes no sense. *For the probability and the degree of assurance are by the nature of the case exactly the same thing.*

There are, however, distinct oddities in Hume's account of what happens when I find one set of arguments more convicing than another. 'I decide from my feeling', he says. This makes it sound as if something like the following happens: I ask myself: 'Which is the more vivid, my idea of p or my idea of q? I decide that p is more vivid than q. Therefore I decide to believe p.' But if I thus 'decide from my feeling', as distinct from simply *feeling*, then a cogitative act is central to the whole analysis. A thorough-going mechanical theory will have to argue, rather, that what we call 'giving the preference to one argument over another' *simply consists* in a more vivid idea somehow driving out a less vivid idea. If Hume does not say this, it is not merely, I think, because he has momentarily fallen back into the language of the vulgar. Rather, he has a picture in the back of his mind, a picture which he cannot entirely expunge, of a human being's hesitating between two alternative views, uncertain which to accept, and finally deciding between them. That, he is suggesting, is not a decision about the strength of evidence but rather a decision about vividness. To leave it entirely out of account would be to do altogether too much violence to the facts.

As Hume's argument proceeds we begin to wonder, furthermore, whether he does *in fact* identify probability with degree of assurance. As I interpret Hume, this is one of the points at which there is a conflict between Hume the moral scientist— Hume the *mitigated* sceptic—and the Pyrrhonian Hume.

Consider his distinction between 'philosophical' and 'unphilosophical' probability. The ground for such a distinction, one would naturally be inclined to suppose, is that the first, though far from being demonstrative, generates beliefs which are in some sense rational, while the second generates beliefs which we are not justified in holding, which we can be blamed, or at least rebuked, for persisting in. Hume the Pyrrhonian sceptic will not permit us to make any such distinction. Philosophical and unphilosophical probability, he in this spirit argues, involve the same psychological mechanism. In each case all that happens is that our idea is vivified; there is no rational ground for preferring the philosophically vivified idea to the unphilosophically vivified idea. Yet under the head of unphilosophical probability Hume includes what he calls 'prejudice'; his example is a person who having met one dishonest Frenchman firmly believes, in consequence, that all Frenchmen are dishonest. A Pyrrhonian would delight in the conclusion that it is a mere prejudice on our part to condemn beliefs arising in such a fashion as prejudices, since they arise in precisely the same way as what we choose to call our 'justified' beliefs, namely as an idea made vivid by a related impression. But Hume the enlightened, Hume the moral philosopher, would by no means welcome it.

For the moment, I shall not carry this line of interpretation any further. Let us return, rather, to Hume's phrase, 'the belief attending the memory and the senses'. It is more than a little strange to speak of 'belief' in this connection. 'I believe I once went to Cambridge' would normally suggest something quite different from 'I remember going to Cambridge'—an element of hesitancy and doubt, a failure to remember, or at the very least to remember clearly, whether I went there or not. There is a similar element of hesitation, normally, in 'I believe that there is a man on that hill' as compared with 'I can see a man on that hill'. But Hume is arguing that even if we ordinarily suppose that there is a difference of the sort suggested by our choice of language in these instances, our choice of the word 'believe' rather than the word 'remember', this supposition is erroneous; we are believing when we remember or perceive quite as much as when we go beyond what we can either remember or perceive. The word 'remembering' serves only to indicate the kind of belief that is in question, its manner of relation to a previous experience.

To believe, for Hume, is to take something to have occurred (memory or retrodictive causal inference), to be occurring (sensation), or to be about to occur (predictive causal inference). That he thinks of belief in this way explains why, in the *Appendix* passage I have already quoted, when he asks whether believing could consist in annexing another idea to an unbelieved idea and so converting it into a believed idea, the candidates which at once come to his mind for that role as an annexed idea are 'reality' and 'existence', rather than, let us, say 'assurance'. To say that belief is nothing but a vivid idea is, for Hume, to say that taking x to exist, or to be about to exist, or to have existed, is identical with *having a vivid idea of x*.

We need not now describe the difficulties Hume gets into when he tries to give an account of this 'vivacity' or the way in which he gradually works towards the somewhat different view that a belief is 'differently conceived' from other ideas. We can set aside the fact, too, that as his argument proceeds, he offers much narrower definitions of belief, whether as '*a lively idea related to or associated with a present impression*' (T, 96), or as arising only from causation (T, 107).[1] These variations, these differentiations of the genus 'vivid idea', bear witness to the fact that he is not, in every mood, happy to identify 'a poetical enthusiasm' and 'a serious conviction'—as he *did* identify them when he wrote that 'tis not solely in poetry and music, we must follow our taste and sentiment, but likewise in philosophy'. *Serious* convictions, unlike poetic enthusiasm, arise, his second thoughts suggest, only when our belief is associated with a present impression or even, his third thoughts suggest, only when it arises out of causation. But he is not going back on his view that belief, whatever else it is, is a vivid idea; in the *Enquiry* he still suggests that this is at least one way of describing the distinctive character of a belief. For our purposes it does not greatly matter whether it can also be described as an idea 'conceived in a certain manner'—whatever this can mean on a Humean view—or even, as some of the things he says in the *Enquiry* might suggest, as an odd sort of sentiment, rather like love and hate. It is enough that belief, on any such interpretation, is still something which we find ourselves with, which happens to us. So for brevity's sake let us hold fast to the vivacity analysis, with the rider that the alternative expression—'manner of conceiving'—surely suggests that a belief is, after all, cogitative rather than sensitive.

Consider in the light of the 'vivacity' analysis of belief Hume's observations at the very end of Book I of the *Treatise*. He is

[1] Compare pp. 61–64 above.

there asking what general conclusions he can draw from his argument as a whole. 'The *intense* view of these manifold contradictions and imperfections in human reason', he writes, 'has so wrought upon me, and heated my brain, that I am ready to reject all belief and reasoning, and can look upon no opinion even as more probable or likely than another' (T, 268–9). 'I am ready to reject all belief . . .'. What can this possibly mean? It might mean something like this: 'My brain is so heated as a result of my considering contradictions that I no longer have any vivid ideas'. But Hume makes it perfectly clear that this is not at all what he means. He is complaining, ideed, that his ideas are only too intense, only too vivid; otherwise he would have no problems. He has to dine, play back-gammon, converse, make merry with his friends before his sceptical views lose their vividness, turn 'cold and strain'd and ridiculous'. When he is 'ready to reject all belief' this cannot mean, either, that he is ready to stop himself from having any vivid ideas; that is impossible. What he is ready to do is something quite different: 'to look upon no opinion as more probable or likely than another'. And this brings out the fact that having a vivid idea and looking upon an opinion as probable are not after all the same thing.

It is notoriously difficult, of course, to determine what Hume wants to say about the degree to which, when we are philosophising, we can succeed in not believing, or can suspend our belief about, what at other times, so he tells us, we *cannot help* believing—nature not having left to us the decision whether to believe or not to believe.[1] We need only insist upon one fact: Hume certainly presumes that we can at least *question* our beliefs even when they are extremely vivid. So far, as Price argues, his philosophical practice is not consistent with his philosophical theory. For 'questioning a belief' cannot mean asking ourselves whether it is really vivid or is really conceived in a certain manner; that is not the sort of thing that can be doubted. What else can it mean, then, except asking ourselves whether it is *really* probable? So being vivid and being

---

[1] Compare my discussion of Price at p. 148 above.

probable cannot be identical. This same conclusion would seem to follow from another, particularly striking, passage in the *Appendix*. 'A . . . reflexion on *general rules*', he there tells us, 'keeps us from augmenting our belief upon every encrease of the force and vivacity of our ideas' (T, 632). So, it would seem, to believe *p* rather than *q* is not, after all, equivalent to having a more vivid idea of *p* than of *q*; we can have a more vivid idea of *p* and yet not believe it. The scientist, relying on 'general rules', is constantly in this position.

In the less heated atmosphere of the *Enquiry*, Hume's metaphysical agitations are subdued. But at the same time it becomes more and more evident that he does not consistently think of belief as an automatic reaction, over which we have in no sense any control. A long note appended to his discussion 'Of the Reason of Animals' (E, 107) brings out this point very clearly. Its placing is interesting. Hume is ready to ascribe belief to animals. After all, they can remember, anticipate. That, not possessing language, they cannot give assent to propositions might lead some philosophers to conclude otherwise, but not Hume. But is Hume really prepared to say that the beliefs of animals, vivid as they no doubt can be, are in every way as good as the beliefs of human beings? And this can be absorbed into another question: Are the beliefs of one man quite as good as the beliefs of another? Hume is not now prepared to answer 'Yes'. Yet if all probable reasoning is nothing but sensation, there does not seem to be the slightest ground for denying to animals, or to the foolish, beliefs as rational as those of the wisest man. Can Hume, consistently with his theory, avoid this conclusion?

As a sceptic, he might not wish to do so. But in fact he makes the attempt, pointing to not one ground of distinction but many. After lengthy experience, he says, wise men, as a result of having become accustomed to the uniformity of nature, acquire a general habit of arguing from the known to the unknown. After 'even one experiment', they 'expect a similar event with some degree of certainty, where the experiment has been made accurately, and free from all foreign circumstances' (E, 107n). When there is a complication of causes, again, the wise man is better than the foolish man at considering the situation as a whole, seeing what goes with what. The forming of general maxims, too, is a delicate business; unlike the prejudiced, the wise do not allow themselves to be led astray by haste or narrowness of vision. And so on.

So we can certainly say this much at least of Hume; he does not invariably write as if our beliefs were the automatic product of custom. He allows that a wise man, when he encounters p, can expect r rather than q because he has examined the situation carefully, not just because r is more vivid than q. So far, at least, belief can be cogitative rather than sensitive. But this still leaves it open to Hume to argue that, once the wise man has done his examining, his idea of r is automatically vivified—even if not, it would seem, by any of the processes Hume has explicitly described—without his having any power to prevent this from happening.

If, on this interpretation, a man may lie open to moral censure for believing r rather than q, it will be for the reason Locke most often suggests: he has not looked carefully enough; he has failed to examine the situation as adequately as he should have done. Even in this case, Hume further suggests, the fact that some men are better endowed than others, have better powers of attention, observation and memory, has the consequence that to blame men for holding r rather than q would be like blaming an animal because it cannot predict an eclipse. But this is surely not the whole story. For it does not seem possible to explain, purely in terms of natural endowments, why some attentive and observant men, confronted by a particular set of evidence, accept it as a proper foundation for believing q and others do not. Wisdom is not the same thing as having good 'faculties' of the sort Hume has enumerated.

Now at long last we reach the crucial passage: 'a wise man proportions his belief to the evidence'. But before examining it, let us look first at the immediately preceding sentences: 'Some events are found, in all countries and all ages, to have been constantly conjoined together: Others are found to have been more variable, and sometimes to disappoint our expectations; so that, in our reasonings concerning matter of fact, there are all imaginable degrees of assurance, from the highest certainty to the lowest species of moral evidence' (E, 110). If this stood alone, we could read it in terms of the mechanical theory. Those conjunctions which are invariable, we might take Hume to be arguing, produce extremely vivid ideas in us—we have a vivid idea of the effect whenever the cause occurs; other conjunctions are more variable and therefore produce less vivid ideas. 'Our reasonings concerning matters of fact' should then be read, in the spirit of Pyrrhonian scepticism, as *what we are pleased to call our reasonings*.

Then, however, it would be absurd to go on and say that 'the wise man proportions his belief to the evidence'. Let us attempt a Humean translation. 'A wise man is one the liveliness of whose ideas correlates with variations in his experience'. But on the interpretation we offered above, this correlation applies to *everyone's* beliefs, to foolish beliefs as much as to the beliefs of the wise, to animal beliefs as much as to human beliefs. To translate in such a manner, then, would be entirely to rule out the obviously intended contrast between the wise man and the foolish man. On the face of it, it is only if we are being called upon to think of the wise man as one who has first looked at the evidence and then *decided* what to believe—or at least how strongly to believe—that Hume is telling us anything at all distinctive about wise men.

It is interesting to observe that this pronouncement about the 'wise man' prefaces Hume's discussion of miracles, interesting because in discussing miracles Hume is talking about the class of beliefs which most concerned Locke, those in which we accept, or reject, somebody's testimony. (Where Hume's cautionary remarks for inquirers have so far turned around the analysis of causes, Locke's, for the most part, turn around the criticism of witnesses.[1]) No doubt, half-realising that he has

[1] Not entirely, of course. But, as I have said, for the most part. Compare Locke's *Essay*, IV, xv, 4.

shifted his ground, Hume attempts to assimilate arguments from testimony to causal arguments. To readers who not unnaturally boggle at this assimilation he replies in a notably off-hand manner: 'I shall not dispute about a word' (E, 111). It is enough, on this view, that just as there is no necessary connection between cause and effect, so too there is no necessary connection between a testimony and its truth. If we still do not care to say that the testimony *causes* its truth, this is a purely verbal quibbling. But in fact a good deal more is involved than verbal usage. For it is a most implausible view that we come to accept testimonies only as a result of having experienced a constant conjunction between testimonies of that type and the truth. Implausible in terms of Hume's general theory; what exactly is 'the truth' in such a conjunction? Empirically implausible, too. At first, in fact, a child automatically believes what he is told; what he acquires as a result of experience is a tendency to be more critical of testimony, more hesitant in accepting it.

Hume recognises, indeed, that our initial tendency is to accept testimony. We have, he says, 'a remarkable propensity to believe whatever is reported . . . however contrary to daily experience and observation' (T, 113). But just how remarkable this propensity is, on his assimilation of arguments from testimony to causal inferences, he does not pause to consider. For his real concern, once more, is with the procedures of the wise, with those who *resist* this propensity.

There is another difference between beliefs arising from testimony and beliefs arising from constant conjunction. When we are suspicious about a testimony, we do not proceed to examine it with the help of the rules Hume lays down for 'judging of causes and effects'. We consider, as Hume himself tells us, the character of the witnesses, the initial plausibility of what they say, their remoteness in time from the events and so on. If it be replied, as Hume replies, that in doing so we rely on such experience-based maxims as are implicitly appealed to in 'The lady doth protest too much, methinks', these maxims, once more, are not causal; the falsity of what the lady says is in no sense a *consequence* of her multiple protesting to the contrary. No doubt, we may come to believe that what she says is false as a consequence of her protesting so much. Nevertheless, the maxim 'those who protest too much often make false statements' is not itself a causal maxim.

In the special case of miracles, so Hume tells us, what I do is to ask myself whether it is more probable that the witness should either be deliberately deceiving me, or should himself have been deceived, than that the events he describes should really have occurred.[1] 'I weigh the one miracle against the other; and according to the superiority, which I discover, I pronounce my decision, and always reject the greater miracle' (E, 116). This is Lockeian in tone; there are two sets of probabilities, I weigh one against the other, discover that one is superior to the other and then . . .

What follows the 'and then'? Hume is sufficiently definite: 'I pronounce my decision'. If this is the right way of putting it, then I *decide* to believe that the testimony is false rather than that the miracle occurred. Admittedly, he continues thus: 'If the falsehood of his testimony would be more miraculous, than the event which he relates; then, and not till then, can he pretend to command my belief or opinion'. This might suggest that once we look at the facts, they determine the outcome, leave us unable to make any decision, that they command us to believe in a particular way. But what, then, is the force of 'pretend' in 'pretend to command'? Does it not suggest '*properly* command'? If so, then Hume is saying that we *ought not* to prefer the testimony to the beliefs we have derived from experience, that, indeed, the wise man will not do so.

Let us take still another look at Hume's description of what happens. 'I weigh the one against the other', the testimony against the likelihood. Who is this 'I'? Hume is certainly not describing, purely and simply, what he himself does as an individual. Just as when he wrote a little earlier that 'we

---

[1] This is a misleading short-hand account of what Hume says, but detail would be out of place here. See, for that detail, Antony Flew: *Hume's Philosophy of Belief*, New York, 1961, ch. VIII.

frequently hesitate concerning the reports of others' (E, 112), he is a spokesman for the wise man—that wise man who lends 'a very academic faith to every report which favours the passion of the reporter' (E, 125). A Pyrrhonian is, in principle at least, an egalitarian; for him one view is as good as another. But in the jargon of our own days, Hume was an élitist. Although there are points at which he sceptically writes as if the wise and the foolish were in exactly the same position, passive victims of their experience, this, as we have already seen, is not at all his invariable opinion. In this section of the *Enquiry*, it is not his opinion at all. Then is Hume simply describing the beliefs of those men we choose to call 'wise'? We choose to call 'wise' those men whose ideas are enlivened by constant conjunctions, we choose to call 'foolish' those men whose beliefs have other sources. That is the end of it.

At certain points in the *Treatise* Hume tries to adopt this merely descriptive attitude: he is the elegant eighteenth-century spectator, contemplating from his coffee-house the strange antics of the passers-by. Or if we like, he is the phenomenologist telling us what is included in our concept of wisdom. But if this were the whole story, his enterprise would be pointless. For he is *arguing against* those who accept miracles; he is exhorting the 'wise and learned', the 'judicious and knowing', to become more sceptical. True enough, he would not expect to convert 'the vulgar'; like Gibbon, he has a strong sense of 'man's knavery and folly'. But if his arguments are valid, then it will be wrong for the wise, at least, to accept as decisive any testimony in favour of miracles.

Confronted by Clifford's dictum that 'it is wrong always, everywhere, and for everyone, to believe anything upon insufficient evidence', Hume might, in his more sceptical moods, reply: 'Evidence is sufficient if in fact it induces men to believe; to say that it is wrong for men to believe on insufficient evidence is to say that it is wrong for them to believe in circumstances in which it is just not possible for them to believe'. But at other times, and especially in the *Enquiry*, his reply would be very different. The vulgar, he would then say, do not examine evidence; their beliefs are entirely the product of 'education'. It is not *wrong* for them to believe on insufficient evidence; that is how they are made. But the wise, if only as a result of experience, develop critical principles, 'general rules'[1], which enable them to proportion their belief to the evidence. At this point, however, 'the evidence' does not mean simply 'that which automatically engenders vivid ideas'. The wise resist the influence of their education, they resist vivid but implausible stories, they weigh alleged evidence before accepting it. And if they do not do this they act wrongly. For 'there is a degree of doubt, and caution, and modesty, which, in all kinds of scrutiny and decision, ought for ever to accompany a just reasoner' (E, 162). *Their* convictions ought to be 'serious', not merely 'poetical enthusiasms' (T, 631).

In the end then, Price seems to be right. If men's beliefs were as automatic as Hume sometimes suggests, if they were always, purely and simply, the product of custom operating upon the imagination, many of Hume's philosophical procedures would be quite fruitless. There are times, certainly, when he suggests that this, by their very nature, is their fate; inevitably, we shall in the end ignore what he has taught us, submitting to our senses and 'understanding' (T, 269). It is certainly no part of his object to convert men in general into sceptical philosophers, especially those honest country gentlemen who represented Hume's social ideal—'employ'd in their domestic affairs, or amusing themselves in common recreations' (T, 272). But he *does* want to destroy superstition; if philosophy is often ridiculous, so he tells us, superstition is both ridiculous and dangerous. That is precisely what leads him to write as if it is both possible and desirable to stand back from our vivid ideas, to decide, in certain circumstances, not to count them amongst our beliefs.

Hume, one might then say, is trying to persuade us to adopt a 'belief policy': the policy of examining critically all beliefs which arise from such suspect sources as 'education', i.e. our upbringing. To that degree he is suggesting that however

---

[1] For some of the problems here see pp. 62–4 above.

vivid an idea may be, we ought sometimes to be prepared to set it aside, temporarily at least. Thus to set it aside is not, of course, the same thing as deciding to believe its contrary. But it does mean that belief lies to some measure under our control; we can deliberately prevent ourselves from believing, even when our education strongly tempts us to believe. And this is how we *ought* to behave. Those who adopt a different policy, for example the policy of accepting whatever they are told, are properly subject to censure. So far, at least, Hume defends an 'ethics of belief'.

INDEX